GEORGE CRABBE
AND THE PROGRESS OF
EIGHTEENTH-CENTURY
NARRATIVE VERSE

GEORGE CRABBE
AND THE PROGRESS OF
EIGHTEENTH-CENTURY
NARRATIVE VERSE

Beth Nelson

LEWISBURG
BUCKNELL UNIVERSITY PRESS
LONDON: ASSOCIATED UNIVERSITY PRESSES

©1976 by Associated University Presses, Inc.

Associated University Presses, Inc.
Cranbury, New Jersey 08512

Associated University Presses
108 New Bond Street
London W1Y OQX, England

Library of Congress Cataloging in Publication Data

Nelson, Beth, 1926–
 George Crabbe and the progress of eighteenth-century
narrative verse.

 Bibliography: p.
 Includes index.
 1. Crabbe, George, 1754–1832—Criticism and
interpretation. I. Title.
PR4514.N4   821'.7   75-5147
ISBN 0-8387-1736-5

PRINTED IN THE UNITED STATES OF AMERICA

to

Josephine Miles

CONTENTS

7

ACKNOWLEDGMENTS

I wish to thank the following publishers for permission to quote from copyrighted material:

Cambridge University Press, *Poems by George Crabbe*, edited by A. W. Ward, 1905–7.
Clarendon Press, Oxford, *The Correspondence of Alexander Pope*, 5 vols., edited by George Sherburn, 1956.
Rinehart and Co., New York and Toronto, *Caleb Williams, or, Things as They Are*, by William Godwin, edited by George Sherburn, 1960.
Routledge and Kegan Paul, London, *Tales and Novels*, by Maria Edgeworth, 1893.

In addition, I wish to thank the National Portrait Gallery in London for permission to reproduce Sir Francis Chantrey's sketch of Crabbe.

I also wish to thank the staff members of the North Library, British Museum; of the Norlin Library, University of Colorado, Boulder; of the libraries of the University of California at Berkeley and Davis. I am particularly indebted to Lucy A. Martin, formerly of the Sacramento State College Library.

9

I am especially grateful to Henry Pettit, Emeritus Professor of English at the University of Colorado, for his careful and helpful reading of the manuscript, and to Paul Levitt, Charles Proudfit, and Constance Wright for encouragement over a long period of time. I also wish to thank Harold Kelling and the English Department of the University of Colorado for making funds available for the typing of the manuscript of this book.

In the early stages of my work, Louis and Helen Knight proved that friendship is still a heroic virtue; my debt to them is beyond acknowledgment. This book is dedicated to the person to whom everything is due.

GEORGE CRABBE
AND THE PROGRESS OF
EIGHTEENTH-CENTURY
NARRATIVE VERSE

1

A QUESTION OF GENRES

In his own time George Crabbe was regarded as a major if disconcerting and suspect poet. Since then, neither the originality of his poetic experiments nor the truthfulness of his representations of life has saved his work from the consequences of too many carelessly written lines and his indifference to 'the integrity of the English sentence. Major or minor, in one age or another, he represents what Henry James would have recognized as an interesting case. He was the last Augustan,[1] the servant of what Rachel Trickett has called the honest muse,[2] a practitioner of a tradition that was outdated even in his own time. As the last Augustan satiric poet writing well into the nineteenth century, Crabbe was an isolated figure, undertaking ingenuous experiments in the service of literary values that he accepted early in his apprenticeship to the satirist Pope, and no experiment of his is more radical or more ingenious than his fusing the novel of the 1790s with the short verse tales of the eighteenth century.

In turning to the novel, Crabbe followed instincts indubitably sound, for here was to be found what could be salvaged of Augustan verse satire, the truthful representa-

tion of the minds and manners of daily life. Behind him
stand the large figures of Fielding, Richardson, and Sterne,
but his back is turned to them. He looks, instead, to his
contemporaries among the novelists—William Godwin,
Elizabeth Inchbald, Maria Edgeworth—as his narrative
poetry looks to the as-yet-unwritten novels of Eliot, Trollope, and James. If his problem was unprecedented, so then
was his solution. It marks him as an eccentric, even among
his contemporaries—the conservative poet, who, in his determination to survive as an artist, ventures on extreme,
seemingly improbable measures that reflect his dilemma
and his times.

Crabbe's call to be a poet was genuine, heard and followed among conditions inimical to the undertaking: he
was provincial, self-taught, impoverished. Even so, he
began to write poetry as a boy, after having chanced to read
some magazine verses; with the help of Pope's Homer, a
rhyming dictionary, and a book on the art of poetry, he
taught himself to write.[3] He began with songs to Delia and
attempted a graveyard poem, but the real bent of talent,
experience, and training soon showed itself when he
privately published "Inebriety," an epical burlesque on
low life. He was then in his twenty-first year.[4] From that
time, he adhered to the doctrine that poetry was an
art that imitated in metrical language actions, passions,
and objects: its range was nearly unlimited; even the
disgusting—in its place—was admissible, for if divine matters were usually above the poet's reach, little was beneath
it. During the course of the eighteenth century, however,
another view first complicated and then undermined these
assumptions by substituting the value of responsiveness for
the value of truthfulness. The newer doctrine encouraged a
poetry of greater intensity and elevation, but it also nar-
rowed the working range of poetry, for if nothing was
above the poet's reach, much was now beneath it. The
merely disgusting or commonplace was no longer suitable
on any terms, and satire was a blot on human nature. In

1754, the year of Crabbe's birth, the respectability of the genre of verse satire, embodied in Pope's reputation, was largely undisputed, although already questioned by some; but by 1785, satiric poetry clearly had no future—and no present. The essence of Crabbe's problem is that, reared in the provinces and self-educated as a poet, he had trained himself during the 1770s in the purposes and methods of verse satire and his work was out-of-date before he began publishing it.

After years of poverty, Crabbe, in a last attempt to continue in his vocation, sought and gained the patronage of Edmund Burke. With the publication of "The Library" in 1781, when Crabbe was twenty-seven years old, his career finally got underway. "The Village" appeared in 1783, corrected, praised, and sponsored by Samuel Johnson in his last act as a critic of English poetry. In 1785 another satire, "The Newspaper," was published; then Crabbe abruptly withdrew from publication for twenty-two years, from 1785 until 1807, in an extended and telling silence.

The three poems of the 1780s are surveys, the first, as it were, of bookshelves, the second of the people in an impoverished village, and the third of kinds of newspapers, their producers, and readers. What informs each of these poems is the author's determination to tell the truth about classes of men as about classes of books and journals: he exposes pretensions, lays bare delusions, praises virtue, and lashes vice in the accepted manner of the satirist. Yet his choices are odd, for in creating an explicit frame for each poem, he required of himself a consistency of subject, treatment, and organization that was not the necessary task of the satirist to provide, working as this kind of poet traditionally did with the wide-ranging, loosely formed *satura*, the mixed dish ready to offer any- and everything. Crabbe had assumed the responsibilities of the satirist early in his career, yet he seems to have enjoyed none of the customary allowances. The attitude was there, the materials were ready, but the old genre was missing.

From Pope's death until the appearance of Churchill in the early 1760s, there was no major poetic satirist in England except Johnson of the Juvenalian imitations; from Churchill's death in 1764 until the publication of "The Village" in 1783, there was no major verse satire published in England. It is true that a large number of satires were produced after 1764, but they were shoddy in design and execution. It is true, too, that major poets wrote satires, but these are among their minor works, and although satirical passages are to be found in major poems, these are passages, not poems. What one will not find is a major satire by a major poet.[5] By 1785 many Englishmen believed that the genre of satire was no longer a serious alternative for a serious poet. Its conventions no longer "worked."

The fictions of the book-lined walls of a library, the format of a newspaper, the class structure of late eighteenth-century rural England, and, later, the pages of a parish register and the epistles of a borough resident, were, like the verse tale, solutions that Crabbe fashioned to meet an abiding and overriding problem, the need for structural principles that would give his poems coherence. His was the same doctrine that the satirist Pope had accepted, but Crabbe was the last eighteenth-century poet to adapt it to the manners and preferences of his own time. In this respect, the liability of being a latter-day verse satirist had its value, for it gave Crabbe a major problem, and insofar as he solved it, he is entitled to be called a serious, an important writer.

His twenty-two year withdrawal from publication is evidence enough that he was fully conscious of the severity of his difficulties. It was not that he had exhausted his subjects: "Numberless were the manuscripts which he completed; and not a few of them were never destined to see the light."[6] Isolation, domestic troubles, and his duties as a clergyman probably contributed to his silence, but I think that the leading cause of his withdrawal lay in his uncertainty about what he was doing and where he was going as a poet. Crabbe had survived the tradition of poetry that had taught and sponsored him. It is no more than a coincidence that Dr. Johnson's death preceded Crabbe's silence by only a year, but it is a significant coincidence. He found that he was solitary. He tried to change and worked on religious and patriotic themes—that is, he essayed the sublime—but he could not write in that manner and gave it up. During the 1790s he began to write narratives in prose and verse. At that time he prepared a volume of verse tales for publication, but at the last minute changed his mind and did not publish.[7] During those years he also wrote three novels but soon destroyed them (Crabbe, Jr., *Life*, p. 47).

At last, in 1807, Crabbe resumed publication with a volume entitled *Poems*, a collection of old and new works, including "The Parish Register," an account of births, marriages, and deaths in a rural village. He returned to his practices of the 1780s, employing his characteristic framing device and the character, anecdote, and progress of Augustan satire, but now he analyzed in detail the minds as well as the manners of village life. In 1810 he published *The Borough*, a collection of epistles representing—again, in character, anecdote, and progress—the classes, occupations, amusements, and institutions of a seaport town. Toward the end of *The Borough* Crabbe suddenly dropped the fiction of the epistle and presented four tales. In these tales as well as in those of *Tales in Verse* (1812) and *Tales of the Hall* (1819) he continued to work with the minds and manners of ordinary life and to hold the truthful mirror of art up to the times, but now he adapted these subjects to the generic and structural demands of the verse tale. Pope's Atossa or Dryden's Zimri, if reduced to the circumstances of a provincial sitting room and if given a narrative line to follow, would not be out of place in one of Crabbe's tales; but it is important that they be given a narrative line, for, in turning to the verse tale, Crabbe had to meet new conditions and consider new literary alternatives. Satire had given way beneath him, and he had to find or invent another poetic kind if he was to continue writing poetry. He settled upon the verse tale, and from 1810 until his death in 1832 he was preeminently a writer of short verse tales.

Given all this, it is no wonder that Crabbe's poetry stands by itself; he is indeed a poet difficult to place—belonging clearly in one century, he published most of his work in the next. He begins as one kind of poet and ends as another, invariably out of step with his times. Or is he actually that much out of step? He didn't want to be. He is therefore a tempting problem to critics and scholars. Some scholars have tried to understand his work by treating it by and for itself, separating it from the complications and disturbances of literary history; others have tried to discern how, over a long period of time, Augustan literary principles developed into the devices of Crabbe's narrative poetry. Many have tried to establish the exact degree of Crabbe's debt to the Augustan poets; a few have tried to establish with equal exactitude but less success the degree to which he was a romantic. What I am attempting to do in this book is rather different, that is, to understand the principles of Crabbe's narrative art by considering his work within the context of certain eighteenth-century narrative traditions. In one sense, I see his effort to write verse tales as an attempt to adapt the Augustan satiric tradition to the preferences and expectations of his own time; in another sense, and it does not undercut the first, the verse tale he contrived represents an adaptation of novelistic intentions, materials, and methods to the short verse tale of the eighteenth century. The verse tales of Crabbe that I shall examine here are those he published in *Poems, The Borough, Tales in Verse,* and *Tales of the Hall,* the volumes that Crabbe himself saw through the press; I have excluded *Posthumous Tales* because of the numerous editorial revisions that Lockhart and Crabbe's son made in Crabbe's text.

In the loose terms of the present century, Crabbe's narratives are *psychological* and *realistic*, as the most casual of his readers may easily gather. This concern with the interacting inevitabilities of mind and external reality dominates his poetry, especially his verse tales. It marks his affinity with those contemporaries who produced a certain kind of prose fiction; it also separates his work from the verse tales of his predecessors and contemporaries. The choices we see an artist make can tell us much about his purposes and methods, and in this respect the ways not taken are sometimes almost as informative as those taken. The short verse tale that Crabbe began publishing in 1810 is the last of his experiments and is itself the eclectic product of his work with already-established narrative kinds. Crabbe's verse tale is in part a novelty, in part an anachronism. In the whole work of any artist there will be a few modes or patterns or a single one that may be called characteristic. Even in the words *realistic* and *psychological* much is already implied. The pattern of Crabbe's tales is that of a lifetime, an internal history shaped and directed by the turns that life is most likely to take, a combination of mutually generating passions and habits, feelings and thoughts, that shift, change, and adapt themselves as they encounter processes equally subtle—social, physiological, historical, economic—implacable realities of a world external, yet related, to character.

What finally sets Crabbe's verse tales apart from others written before or during his time is this pattern, and it is this that his work holds in common with the novel. Yet this characteristic distinguishes his narrative practice; it does not exhaust it. On the contrary, as a narrative poet, Crabbe had clearly defined alternatives—well-established verse-narrative kinds and methods a century old. There was the novel, definitively; there was also the verse tale, a little-known because little-regarded province of eighteenth-century poetry.

The verse tale that Crabbe knew, largely rejected, and yet was beholden to was an old genre, widely practiced in the eighteenth century by poets good and bad alike. Every important eighteenth-century anthology included verse tales and nearly every important poet wrote at least one or two, while minor and less-than-minor writers brought them forth in depressingly large numbers—moral tales, smutty tales, elevated tales that imitated the ballad or sought more modern and more pathetic effects. Prior, Parnell, Congreve, Swift, Pope, Gay, Thomson, Shenstone, Ramsay, Cowper, Goldsmith, Scott, Burns, Blake, Percy, and, among those whose first names are necessary, Anna Seward, Edmund Cartwright (yes, the inventor), Robert Bloomfield all worked in one way or another with the verse tale. There were, for these writers, two clearly recognized and very different genres, and all of these poets worked within the clearly defined limits of these kinds. The first of these, the preceptive tale, was intended to instruct and relied upon plot to realize that end.[8] It invariably offered a precept, whether stated or implied; usually the tale began or ended with a maxim out of which the action grew or toward which it tended. The other kind, which I shall call the pathetic tale, was designed to arouse the reader's passions, not to instruct. Its creator relied on declamation as a sure stimulus of feeling.

In order to understand the art of Crabbe's own verse tale, it will be necessary to consider these two eighteenth-century genres in some detail and to compare Crabbe's methods to those of the preceptive and pathetic narrative poets. Because very little work has been done with the short verse tale of the eighteenth century, I shall have to spend more time with it than at first might seem necessary in a work on Crabbe. Before one can understand the significance of what Crabbe did or did not do, one must know what he had to work with and to work against, to exploit or to repudiate; and the discussion of preceptive and pathetic tales, as it illuminates Crabbe's practice, throws its own light, too, on the theory and practice of literature in the eighteenth century.

Crabbe often mined the verse tales of the eighteenth century for the "groundwork" of his own tales; he was well acquainted, it is evident, with the most important verse tales of that century, but the transformations he effected on what he appropriated were drastic. He lowered the subject matter and internalized what he had received as external, amplified where others had concentrated, and foreshortened where they had elaborated. The short verse tale that he produced between 1810 and 1820, and that he continued to write until his death in 1832, represents an action of the mind in a plot designed to accord with "the real tendency of things." It deals with the lower and middle walks of life; it is imitative and analytic in its methods, sympathetic in its attitude, and morally instructive in its end. He required, he said, that his tales be "brief" and "singular," but not too "interesting," for the "principal incident" must not leave the reader's mind too "lacerated."[9] His tales must be about "really existing creatures," not "beings of my own imagination": "I do not know," he said, "that I could paint merely from my own fancy, and there is no cause why I should. Is there not diversity sufficient in society?"[10] The aesthetic basis of his work is truth, not beauty, and we must look to the novel for its counterpart.

I have already mentioned the three novels that Crabbe wrote and destroyed during the 1790s. The logic of Crabbe's interest in the novel is apparent when one considers what was being published during this decade. Among the poets, the works of Burns, Blake, Bowles, Darwin, Rogers, and Campbell frequently appeared, but Crabbe was no lyricist nor sublime enthusiast, nor, given his interest in minds and manners, could he have found assurance in the loves of the plants or in elegiac sunsets. The pleasures of hope and memory were congenitally alien to him, as were the Gothic assumptions of versified tales of terror. The notable publications of poetry during this period are of course the early works of the romantics—the beginnings of another kind of poetry that remained inaccessible and inexplicable to Crabbe. Isolated in a country parish, Crabbe witnessed drastic changes in poetic preferences that were hostile to his art, and I think he grew unsure of the validity of his own work. However, the situation is very different for prose fiction. Two kinds were dominant, the Gothic, which Crabbe distrusted, and social-psychological fiction, with which Crabbe's narrative poetry has important affinities. William Godwin, Elizabeth Inchbald, Thomas Holcroft, and, as a precursor of Maria Edgeworth and others, Mary Wollstonecraft—all of them radicals—were then publishing novels and prose tales. They represented "man as he is" and "things as they are" and delineated the operations of the mind in the real world. Accordingly, they are Crabbe's real contemporaries, and the poets are not. It is not surprising that Crabbe turned to the novel, for here he found writers whose literary intentions agreed with his own.

Later, the work of some of these novelists will be examined, and what will then appear is that what they were doing in prose fiction Crabbe was later to attempt within the narrow limits of the short verse tale. Eighteenth-century moral—that is, psychological—theory had defined, as the following chapter will indicate, the process of passions operating on the mind—that activity of the powers of remembering, imagining, reasoning, and willing.[11] Crabbe, like the novelists, appropriated this theory, using it as the central principle of his verse tale. The radical novelists, like Crabbe, represented man as he is and things as they are, and to do so, they broke with the conventional method of ordering plot—poetic justice, which arranges things as they ought to be, not as they are—and thus changed the pace and direction of narrative. Fiction assumed the burden of telling the truth of what came of the interaction of mental process and the forces of the real world. In the novels of the 1790s and in Crabbe's tales the values of a new kind of fiction were being defined, the same kind of fiction that Eliot, Trollope, and James were to write. The inner histories of Dorothea Brooke or Lydgate—like those of Lizzie Eustace and Maggie Verver—converge with their time and class and attract and gather round themselves the moral histories and destinies of other characters until one complex pattern is formed, a comprehensive representation of social and moral life. The Victorian novel had what Crabbe sought all his life as a poet, a coherent structure that registers freely and fully in analysis, description, and dialogue the subtle changes that accompany a lifetime's moral history in a complicated and uncontrollable external world. What, in the end, affords the real interest of George Crabbe's case is how unerringly he selected from the wreck of his tradition the fragments that were to provide the foundation for the major literary achievement of the next hundred years.

2

THEORIES

It is well known that during the second half of the eighteenth century there was a gradual but visible, confused and confusing shift from a poetic based on imitation to one based on expression. The signs of this change appeared early, and its consequences were carried over into the following century and on into our own.[1] Of course George Crabbe felt the effects of this change, for the basis of his art was imitation; still, his was not so much the imitation of general nature, which was the province of the poet of the higher kinds, as it was the imitation of nature, particularly human nature, in its daily particularities, the "low" subject of satire, comedy, and the novel. The traditional justification for Crabbe's accurate realism and his detailed psychological studies was that these representations, though low, are true, and men will be entertained and instructed by them. For Crabbe, actuality, not ideality, was the substance of poetry, and morality, not rapture, its end; as a poet, he thought he should represent the turns and movements of heart and mind and to judge the represented actions:

For this the poet looks the world around,
Where form and life and reasoning man are found.
He loves the mind in all its modes to trace,
And all the manners of the changing race;
. . . .
He finds what shapes the Proteus-passions take,
And what strange waste of life and joy they make,
And loves to show them in their varied ways,
With honest blame or with unflattering praise.
'Tis good to know, 'tis pleasant to impart,
These turns and movements of the human heart;
The stronger features of the soul to paint,
And make distinct the latent and the faint;
Man, as he is, to place in all men's view.[2]

(ll. 426–40)

For a growing number of poets, critics, and mere readers, these were not the grounds of "genuine" poetry, nor was one necessarily an adherent of the expressive doctrine to think so. It was Crabbe's misfortune to learn early in his career that he was practicing an old-fashioned art and to learn later that, no matter how hard he might try, he could practice no other.

In large part, Crabbe's troubles as a poet were the consequence of the decline of the genre system, a decline related, as Meyer Abrams has shown, to the failing authority of the doctrine of imitation (pp. 145–46). During the eighteenth century the genre of satire steadily lost its traditional prestige and safeguards; it is not sublime and can not be pathetic enough to stand on its own merits. Under the old system, all agreed that the epic was a greater genre than satire, but all also assumed that a work of art could be judged only by the rules of its own kind, not those of a higher genre. Satire is low—with Horace as the authority, who would deny it? None of the "neoclassical" critics supposed that a verse satire could compete in emotional power with *Paradise Lost* or Pindar's odes; Boileau, following

Horace, defined satire as an imitation of contemporary life directed toward moral ends:

> Desire to show it self, and not to wrong
> Arm'd Virtue first with Satyr in its Tongue,
> *Lucillius* was the Man who bravely bold,
> To *Roman* Vices did this Mirror hold,
> Protected humble Goodness from reproach,
> Show'd Worth on Foot and Rascals in the Coach.[3]

The satirist holds the mirror up to his times and reveals vices that ought to be condemned and virtues that deserve praise. The mixed dish of satire, in the urbane style of its own time, appropriately harsh in its measure, is circumstantial and particular in its painting of a familiar world:[4] "Though distant times may rise in satire's page, / Yet chief 'tis hers to draw the present age . . ." (ll. 239–40).[5] As Pope says, "In this impartial Glass, my Muse intends / Fair to expose myself, my Foes, my Friends; / Publish the present Age . . ." (ll. 57–59).[6] The materials of the satirist are the manners of his own time; it is perhaps for this reason that, barring burlesque and mock-heroic, no modernizations of the *Iliad* or the *Aeneid* were produced, whereas some of the best poetry written in the eighteenth century—for example, Pope's Horatian and Johnson's Juvenalian imitations —recast ancient into modern manners.

Soon enough, however, the opinion grew that the poet who proceeded in the manner Boileau had described wrote something more like prose than poetry, for he dealt with familiar manners and morality, not with impassioned expression and impassioned response. The destruction of Boileau's reputation in England was completed long before the end of the eighteenth century; the destruction of Pope's followed more slowly.[7] Joseph Warton, as Paul Leedy has shown, ignored the distinctions of the traditional genre system when he concluded that because "Wit and Satire are transitory and perishable, but Nature and Passion are eternal," a satire is an inferior genre and the Pope of that genre is a poet of the second rank. Warton had helped to begin a movement that would end by declaring not merely that satirical poems are by nature second rate but that they are not poetry at all.[8] Pope, as a satirist, had "stuck to describing *modern manners,* but those *manners,* because they are *familiar, uniform, artificial,* and *polished,*" are "in their very nature, unfit for any lofty effort of the Muse," and the lofty Muse was becoming synonymous with "genuine" poetry. Reading one of Pope's satires "affects not our minds with such strong emotions as we feel from *Homer* and *Milton;* so that no man of a true poetical spirit, is *master of himself while he reads* them."[9] The strength or weakness of the eighteenth-century reader's emotional response determined a poem's merits, finally determined whether it was or was not "poetry."

Warton undervalued satire because it is concerned with "the things that go on all around one day after day."[10] Its effect is limited presumably to the time for which it has been written, whereas "genuine" poetry is written for all men in all times, who are, of course, universally susceptible to sublimity and pathos. A critic less temperate than Warton, William Lisle Bowles carried the argument to its logical extreme in the first decade of the nineteenth century. I believe that no one in the eighteenth century would have quarreled with Bowles's first proposition that passions belonging to "NATURE in general" are better adapted to the "HIGHER SPECIES of Poetry" than are those "derived from *incidental* and transient MANNERS";[11] but Bowles, ignoring differences in genres, goes on to assert that, irrespective of "merit" in execution, Pope's "Eloisa" is *"intrinsically* more *poetical,* than a poem founded on the characters, incidents, and modes of *artificial life;* for instance, the Rape of the Lock." Bowles concludes: "To say that Pope, in this sense, is not a poet, is to say that a *didactic Poem* is not a *Tragedy*, and that *Satire* is not an *Ode";* because *"artificial life"* is the subject of satire, "to say that satire is not poetry, is to say that an epigram is not an elegy" (pp. 7–11, *passim*). The

confusion in Bowles's logic need not detain us, but his conclusion is plain: because satire deals with manners, not with
the permanent general passions, satire is not poetry and the
satirist Pope is not a poet. That Warton's conclusions are
qualified by his respect for Pope's art and that Bowles's
are not suggest the momentum acquired by this opinion between 1760 and 1800.

This change in the evaluation of poets was accompanied
by a corresponding change in literary theory. In 1711
Joseph Trapp defined poetry as a wholly imitative art;[12] in
1789 Thomas Twining found poetry to be imitative only
in certain, very limited respects.[13] As imitation diminished
in authority, passion extended its power. Beginning in 1701
with Dennis's definition of poetry as "an Imitation of Nature, by a pathetick and numerous Speech," the degree of
excellence to be determined by the degree of passion,[14] this
doctrine gathered force until in 1776 Sir William Jones
could declare that poetry in its origins and very nature was
an expressive art;[15] in 1782 Hugh Blair defined poetry as
"the language of passion, or of enlivened imagination,
formed, most commonly, into regular numbers." For Blair,
as his affection for Ossian testifies, the language of passion
meant the language uttered under the immediate influence
of real feeling: the poet's "mind . . . is animated by some
interesting object which fires his imagination, or engages his
passions; and which, of course, communicates to his style a
peculiar elevation suited to his ideas. . . ."[16] How is this then
communicated to the reader? "Enthusiastic and impassioned modes of speech" are "the great vehicles of
sympathy—the sole means of conveying warm and animated sentiments from one mind to another, since that,
which is not expressed with all the energetic glow of real
ecstasy, will never excite any ecstatic feelings in the reader.
. . ."[17] An aroused poet will produce an aroused reader, and
they   communicate   by   Longinian   contagion.   No
eighteenth-century critic or poet of whatever persuasion
would have denied the importance of passion in poetry, but

there is a real difference between imitating passionate speech and regarding poetry as primarily the art of expressing passion. As Abrams has shown, there was a movement during the eighteenth century from a poetic that assumed that poetry was primarily the representation of reality to one that assumed it was the "spontaneous overflow of powerful feelings." The implications are obvious: if a poem is not couched in the language of sincere passion, it is not poetry but versified prose.

In the later years of the century, the contest between poetry as imitation and poetry as the language of passion was fought on the higher ground of general theory, but Crabbe's immediate problem pertained to what he could and could not write. Probably there were many among Crabbe's contemporaries who, if asked, whether poetry is an imitative or an expressive art, would have replied, without too much thought, that it is, of course, imitative; yet in all likelihood these same readers would have added that Crabbe's poetry is not "genuine" because of his subjects and his methods of treating them. Under the genre system the principle of decorum determines what one can or cannot do in a given genre; the writer of epic ought not descend to the low or trifling, nor, unless his intentions are burlesque, should the satirist strive for the heroic or enthusiastic eminence of epic or ode. The higher genres are high because their subjects are universal, that is, actions and reactions characteristic of the general nature of men in all times and places; the lower genres, among them satire, have to do with more particularized circumstances, local and transitory in their nature. Yet a poet can be "low" with impunity—he can deal with daily life and with contemporary topics—as long as he limits himself to certain genres. After the leveling of the genre system, it soon became apparent that he could not be "low" on any occasion and still suppose that what he wrote was genuine poetry. The genre system failed, but the principle of decorum did not; now, unmodified or unrestrained by any complex system of limited ends and means, it became tyrannical, determining not what was appropriate in a certain kind of poem, but what was and what was not poetry. The low, the mean, the trifling, and the disgusting are accidental and transitory and therefore will not appeal to all men in all times. Maternal love is always the same, always elevating the individual to the level of the species, whereas the desire to be lord of the bedchamber is in itself an "artificial" desire contingent on a certain kind of society that is in itself transitory, degrading the man from the natural father to the unnatural courtier. The first is therefore a proper subject of poetry, and the second is not. The writer concerning himself with the first writes poetry; the writer concerning himself with the second does not.

The reader's pleasure becomes the gauge of what the poet can and can not do. In large part, this is the result of eighteenth-century aesthetics, which stressed, not the work of art, but the workings of passion, judgment, fancy, and pleasure and pain in the reader, for the eighteenth century assumed with growing certainty that the laws of art and the laws of the mind are one, and, by nature, man is directed toward pleasure as an end. An earlier reader had derived pleasure from perceiving the resemblance between the imitation and the reality—the pleasure that truth affords[18] —but now the reader found his emotional responses a preeminent pleasure in themselves. Much of actual life is painful—tedious because familiar and lacerating because wretched—and so, inevitably, much of actual life was eliminated from those subjects eligible for genuine poetry.

The traditional justification for the genre of satire is that an accurate representation gives pleasure; its moral justification, that it instructs the reader. It is the satirist's duty to make vice appear as it is—odious or ridiculous—and virtue, lovable, so that the reader, moved by the appropriate passions, will seek virtue and avoid vice.[19] In this way, satire, like the other genres, moves, pleases, and teaches. Dennis insisted that passion in poetry leads swiftly and effectively to the proper end of poetry, improvement of the reader.[20] For Blair, however, "the primary aim of the poet" is "to please and move"; only "indirectly" does he instruct (*Lectures,* p. 511). Earlier, men had assumed that if a poem failed to please and move, it would fail in its essential purpose. In the course of the eighteenth century the reader's pure pleasure in being moved came to determine what a poet could and could not do, and this pleasure had much to do with the doctrine of sympathy. The poet moves the reader by making him feel with and for the characters or the speaker of the poem, for the sympathetic response, even on tragic occasions, affords us pleasure; the lively and sometimes unprecedented "movement" of the reader's feelings relieves the tedium of his usual life[21] and, according to one view, makes possible the "exquisite and refined pleasure" of "self-approbation" that attends the reader's perception of his own "virtuous sympathy."[22] Earlier, the reader had perceived, with pleasure, the resemblance between a representation and the reality; now he looks into himself and sees, with pleasure, his own virtue. The reader's pleasure has become, in effect, the basis for new rules, more general but no less influential than the "rules" of the old genre system. For one thing, the poet in his choice of subjects and his treatment of them must observe a nice balance between moving the reader and moving him perhaps too much. The trouble with real life is that the sufferings exhibited there "excite such a painful degree of sympathy, as would overpower and suppress the pleasant feelings, excited by the noble, tender, or generous sentiments. . . ."[23] Thus the poet, if he is to please his reader, must insure that his subjects and treatment are agreeable, tender, and noble, or he will pain rather than please him. Things as they are and man as he is could have little place under the new dispensation because they prohibit the refined pleasures of sympathy and self-approbation by making the reader feel more on behalf of others than he could comfortably enjoy for himself.

"That the pleasures of poetry arise chiefly from the agreeable feelings which it conveys to the mind by awakening the imagination, is a proposition which may seem too obvious to stand in need of proof."[24] So in 1814 wrote Dugald Stewart, who went on to say that the pleasure produced by the "higher kinds of poetry"—in the view of many the only kind of poetry—arises in part from "that dissatisfaction which the objects of imagination inspire us with, for the scenes, the events, the characters with which our senses are conversant" (2: 468). Therefore, in all "serious productions" the poet's "one great object" is "to elevate the imagination of his readers above the grossness of sensible objects and the vulgarity of common life . . ." (2: 329). To insure agreeable feelings in the reader and to elevate him above the vulgarity of his daily experience, the poet has at his disposal subjects seemingly unlimited: "all the glories of external nature; all that is amiable, or interesting, or respectable in human character; all that excites and engages our benevolent affections; all those truths which make the heart feel itself better and more happy. . . ." In this "world" of poetic choices, "no inconveniences damp our enjoyments, and . . . no clouds darken our prospects" (2: 444).

In this world, too, there is no place for Atossa or Chloe, Peter Grimes or Abel Keene, nor is there any place for satire in general or Crabbe in particular. The author of "Eloisa" is a "serious" or "genuine" poet; the author of the "Moral Epistles" is not. Wordsworth, who sought to make the expressive style a dignified and rational poetic mode, could not admit that Crabbe was a poet. It is true that Wordsworth made "a selection of the language really spoken by men" the principle of his style, but "this selection, wherever it is made with true taste and feeling, will of itself form a distinction far greater than would at first be imagined, and will entirely separate the composition from the vulgarity and meanness of ordinary life. . . ."[25] He assessed Crabbe's work accordingly:

I am happy to find that we coincide in opinion about Crabbe's *verses;* for *poetry* in no sense can they be called.

... At the best, it is the meanest kind of satire, except the merely personal. ... nineteen out of 20 of Crabbe's Pictures are mere matters of fact; with which the Muses have just about as much to do as they have with a collection of Medical Reports.[26]

Coleridge too found Crabbe's work deficient: "Crabbe's poems are founded on observation and real life," and although "he has much power of a certain kind," there is also "an absolute defect of the high imagination; he gives me little or no pleasure. ..."[27] The early nineteenth-century response to Crabbe may be summed up in Fanny Kemble's words: "for a great poet, which he is, he is curiously unpoetical, I think."[28]

Crabbe's vulnerability is obvious, and no one was more aware of it than he. He had tried nobler themes, "but, after many efforts to satisfy myself by various trials on these subjects, I declined all further attempt, from a conviction that I should not be able to give satisfaction to my readers."[29] Instead, when he resumed publication in 1807, he still preferred the "low," the "mean," the "disgusting." Truth has its own value, and there is always the pleasure of resemblance:

> This let me hope, that when in public view
> I bring my pictures, men may feel them true;
> "This is a likeness," may they all declare,
> "And I have seen him, but I know not where."[30]
>
> (ll. 442–45)

He granted that the "effect of poetry should be to lift the mind from the painful realities of actual existence," but he could not understand what the difficulty was:

> But what is there in all this, which may not be effected by a fair representation of existing character? nay, by a faithful delineation of those painful realities, those every-day concerns ... provided they be not ... the very concerns and distresses of the reader?[31]

And, on another occasion,

> I plead not for the originality, but for the truth, of the
> character; and, though it may not be very pleasing, it may
> be useful to delineate (for certain minds) these mixtures
> of levity and vice . . . . These characters demand some
> attention, because they hold out a warning to that
> numerous class of young people who are too lively to be
> discreet.[32]

He justified his work on the grounds of its truth, not its
agreeableness. When he called upon the reader's sympathy,
and he frequently did, self-approbation was not the end he
sought; rather, he asked that the reader, having seen a copy
of the reality, recognize there a human likeness and a fellow
sinner. Trained in verse satire, he represented the minds
and manners of common life, offered praise and blame,
and ultimately justified his art as imitative and useful.

Crabbe, moreover, was aware, even during the period of
his greatest popularity, that the art he practiced was under
attack. He recognized, too, that the repeated attacks on
Pope's satires were directed against the doctrines that
underlay his own poetry. He did not suppose, he wrote in
the preface to *Tales in Verse*, "that by describing as faithfully
as I could, men, manners, and things, I was forfeiting a just
title to a name which has been freely granted to many
whom to equal, and even to excel, is but very stinted com-
mendation." The question of what is and what is not
"genuine poetry" will be determined, he says, by "that
definition of the poetic character" which each man holds;
and, according to one definition of "great authority,"

> the poet is one who, in the excursions of his fancy be-
> tween heaven and earth, lights upon a kind of fairy-land,
> in which he places a creation of his own, where he em-
> bodies shapes, and gives action and adventure to his ideal
> offspring; taking captive the imagination of his readers,
> he elevates them above the grossness of actual being, into

the soothing and pleasant atmosphere of supra-mundane existence: there he obtains for his visionary inhabitants the interest that engages a reader's attention without ruffling his feelings, and excites that moderate kind of sympathy which the realities of nature oftentimes fail to produce, either because they are so familiar and insignificant that they excite no determinate emotion, or are so harsh and powerful that the feelings excited are grating and distasteful.

For the sake of argument, he will "concede" that the poets of fancy and imagination offer a "higher and more dignified composition, nay, the only kind that has pretensions to inspiration":

still, that these poets should so entirely engross the title as to exclude those who address their productions to the plain sense and sober judgment of their readers, rather than to their fancy and imagination, I must repeat that I am unwilling to admit—because I conceive that, by granting such right of exclusion, a vast deal of what has been hitherto received as genuine poetry would no longer be entitled to that appellation.

Clear indeed are the consequences if poets and poetry are to be so narrowly defined:

All that kind of satire wherein character is skilfully delineated must (this criterion being allowed) no longer be esteemed as genuine poetry; and for the same reason many affecting narratives which are founded on real events, and borrow no aid whatever from the imagination of the writer, must likewise be rejected: a considerable part of the poems, as they have hitherto been denominated, of Chaucer, are of this naked and unveiled character. . . . Dryden has given us much of this poetry, in which the force of expression and accuracy of description have neither needed nor obtained assistance from the fancy of the writer; the characters in his Absalom and Achitophel are instances of this. . . . Pope himself has no small portion of this actuality of relation, this nudity of description, and poetry without an atmosphere; the lines beginning, "In the worst inn's worst room," are an example, and many others may be seen in his Satires, Imitations, and above all in his Dunciad: the frequent absence of those "Sports of Fancy," and "Tricks of strong Imagination," have been so much observed, that some have ventured to question whether even this writer were a poet; and though, as Dr. Johnson has remarked, it would be difficult to form a definition of one in which Pope should not be admitted, yet they who doubted his claim, had, it is likely, provided for his exclusion by forming that kind of character for their poet, in which this elegant versifier, for so he must be then named, should not be comprehended.

(2: 9–11, *passim*)

What Crabbe had perceived and what, I believe, had long disturbed him was that the Augustan tradition and satiric poetry were no longer merely questioned, but, rather, discredited as not "serious" or "genuine" poetry; even Jeffrey, still regarded in the late twentieth century as the defender-in-chief of Augustan poetry, dismissed Pope as "a satirist, . . . a wit, and a critic, and a fine writer, much more than he is a poet."[33]

The attacks on Crabbe's poetry in the periodicals of the early nineteenth century have escaped the notice of many of Crabbe's recent critics, who seem to assume that the reviewers were more favorably disposed toward his work than in fact they were; however, these attacks did not escape Crabbe's notice.[34] It was to these critics that he addressed his prefaces, and after reading a number of the reviews of Crabbe's work, one understands why he had to defend himself against charges that arose from an entire misunderstanding of his purposes as a poet.

No early nineteenth-century reviewer was prepared to question Crabbe's talent, but nearly all quarreled with what he had done with it. A few reviewers, such as Jeffrey and the *Monthly's* man, quite justly complained of his careless versification as well as the "harshness" of his numbers.[35] Generally, the critics deplored his choice of subjects—the mean, the trifling, the vile, the loathsome, the disgusting —and they deplored his manner of treating them, particularly the tedious minuteness of his descriptions; but they especially objected to his refusal to accept the poet's natural obligation to elevate.

Jeffrey has been called Crabbe's most "sympathetic" early nineteenth-century critic,[36] as indeed he was; his reviews of Crabbe's work between 1807 and 1819 are intelligent, carefully considered, and eminently fair attempts to assess Crabbe's achievement, but the truth is that Jeffrey, like Hazlitt, felt "disgust" all too often as he read Crabbe's poetry. For Hazlitt, the famous description of the marsh in "Peter Grimes" is "an exact *fac-simile* of some of the most unlovely parts of the creation,"[37] and Jeffrey found Crabbe's characters often too vile for sympathy and too mean to injure any one but themselves.[38] What Jeffrey recognized, and other critics did not, is that in the "painful" and "familiar" Crabbe had ready access to the reader's heart (16: 33–34). As the years went on, Jeffrey still waited for Crabbe to realize the potentialities that the critic had assigned—retrospectively, not initially—to "Sir Eustace Grey": power, passion, elevation, and terror.[39] It was Jeffrey who first called Crabbe the "satirist of low life—an occupation in great degree new and original in our language," but he added, with relief, that much of Crabbe's poetry is of "a higher character" that moves or delights us by its "lively, touching, and finely contrasted representations of dispositions, sufferings, and the occupations of those ordinary persons. . . ."[40] Moreover, Jeffrey found that in *Tales in Verse* Crabbe began to move away from the merely disgusting and the too minutely labored.[41] As Jeffrey and other critics recognized, Crabbe was an original, "distinguished from all other poets, both by the choice of his subjects, and his manner of treating them." His persons come from "the lower ranks of life; and all his scenery from the most ordinary and familiar objects of nature or art."[42]

The response to his work varied from Jeffrey's general approbation and occasional disgust to the "loathing" that afflicted *The Christian Observer* as each new volume of Crabbe's poetry appeared. "It is impossible," said the *Monthly Review* in 1810, "not to lament that a mind thus nervous and powerful should often waste itself in dilating on useless particulars, which are sometimes trifling, and not seldom revolting."[43] The *Quarterly Review*, in the same year, predicted the end of the vogue for Crabbe:

> The first glow of admiration, however, is now gone and sufficient time has since passed to allow of our ascertaining, pretty accurately, the final judgment of the public respecting the merits of Mr. Crabbe. It is, if we are not mistaken, that he has greatly misapplied great powers; and that, although an able, he is not a pleasing poet.[44]

The *Quarterly* continues: "He wishes to discard everything like illusion from poetry"; he is intent on confining himself "with more than ordinary rigour, to truth and nature," an intention that "tends greatly to circumscribe, if not completely to destroy, the operation of illusion in poetry. . . .' Therefore, "the doctrines of Mr. Crabbe appear to us essentially hostile to the highest exercise of the imagination. . . . It is precisely in order to escape from the world as it is, that we fly to poetry" (4: 281–82). Even if Crabbe insists on dealing with "the realities of *low life* . . . of all others, the most disgusting," it is his duty as a poet "to select such of its features as may at least be inoffensive."

> In common life every man instinctively acquires the habit of diverting his attention from unpleasing objects, and fixing it on those that are more agreeable; and all we ask is, that this practical rule should be adopted in poetry. (4: 288)

Crabbe's "knowledge of man is never exhibited on a grand scale. It is clear and exact . . . a knowledge of the individual rather than of the species." Nor is that all: "He admits coarseness on system. . . . His sagacity in the discovery, and his ardour in the pursuit of offensive images are sometimes astonishing. . . . In his pity there seems to be more of contempt than tenderness, and the objects of his compassion are . . . the objects of his satire" (4: 291).

In 1811 *The Christian Observer* said that "the manners and sentiments of the vulgar" have frequently furnished materials to the poet, but until Crabbe appeared these were rendered with "delicacy and *amiableness*"; in Crabbe's poetry one finds, not "the solitary cottage" or "grotto," but the workhouse, with the characters exhibited as he found them "in all their native coarseness and depravity, or in all their simple and unvarnished merit."[45] Rightly has he been called, the reviewer goes on, *"the satirist of low-life,"* and he has applied himself chiefly to "the delineation of character and manners" (10: 503). However, these characters and manners are offensive: "Whatever in low life is most abhorrent and disgusting, vice, infamy, and disease, indigence, insanity, and despair, seem to be eagerly selected by this author. . . ." When not "revolting," his subjects "are often radically mean and uninteresting, such as no moral can exalt, or splendour of fiction adorn." The *Observer* was surprised that Crabbe did as well as he did with his "untractable materials"—proof indeed of his "extraordinary powers." Surely, his choice of subjects was "deliberate," and though Crabbe might argue that in this late age only "the refuse materials of poetry" remain, happily Campbell and Scott prove the fallacy of that argument (10: 510–11).

In 1819 *The Christian Observer* was as wary of Crabbe as ever, "our able and faithful copist of nature in her lowly forms," whose "satiric muse" awakens "chiefly those sensations which arise in reading Pope's Satirical Letters, his Dunciad. . . ." Nor are these the best sensations one can have. Crabbe, for example, is "wholly insensible" of the

"feelings of the genuine and lofty *epic*," and "has gone beyond all his predecessors of name and note . . . in rejecting
the very front or colour of that ambitious style."[46] Does he
please us? the *Observer* asked. No, reviewers have been "lit-
erally writhing under the horrors of the song, and gasping
after terms to express their shocked and severely pained
feelings. . . ." Does he instruct us? the reviewer inquired. No
more than any other satirist. No, he neither pleases nor
truly instructs, for his characters never rise to "a certain
pitch of gigantic action" or sink to a "state of honourable
misfortune." His "favoured objects" are a "set of low, mean,
pitiful, and scoundrel passions, the sordid offerings of pure
selfishness. . . ." The *Observer* found no signs of anything
"great, generous, and godlike." Even Christianity—"we say
it with pain"—is "degraded." Nor do his "effusions" lead us
"to all that is great and noble and generous in our common
nature" and bear us "as on eagle wings, towards heaven."
And Crabbe would do well to teach "less of the love of the
sex, but more of the love of human kind, the love of virtue,
the love of country, the love of God." The reviewer rec-
ommended that Crabbe heed "the angel-flight" of "Mr.
Southey's maturer muse" (18: 657–67, *passim*).

He was not elevated and obviously was far too loyal to the
suspect satire of the Augustans. If the reviewers were sus-
picious of Crabbe for his refusal to produce effusions that
lifted the reader above ordinary life, Crabbe, in his turn,
rejected not only their suggestions but also the principle of
elevated and elevating poetry. In a letter commenting on
the 1819 review in *The Chistian Observer,* Crabbe questioned
the doctrines upheld in the reviews:

> Little I am afraid can be effected by the Muse of most
> moral and even seraphic Endowments: the Urania of Mil-
> ton and the—I know not what to call her—of Young
> included: Creating in the Reader a general sobriety and
> some Elevation of Mind is all I think that can be expected
> or that will be found to arise from the perusal of the more
> serious and sublime poetry, but even if I thought more

might be done, a Writer must consider whether he be capable of doing it. I endeavour to take up the Burden that fits my Shoulders and I fear that under one of the more weighty or precious Kind, I should stumble or fall.[47]

Crabbe was, it seems, by nature not Longinian. He did not make impassioned language the staple of his verse; rather, the passions, to Crabbe, were realities to be represented, not internal forces driving him to song: he analyzed them, traced their processes and represented the consequences of their "waste of joy and life." What Crabbe set out to do as a poet was what Joseph Trapp had earlier said a poet, by definition, must do, for poetry is *"An Art of imitating or illustrating in metrical Numbers every Being in Nature, and every Object of the Imagination, for the Delight and Improvement of Mankind"*; imitation "impresses upon the Mind a true and genuine Representation of any Thing . . . Passions, Things, Places, and Men."[48] Although painting may excel in imitating the objects of sense, the peculiar province of poetry is to paint "the inward Springs and Movements of the Soul, the Actions, Passions, Manners, the distinguishing Tempers and Natures of Men"; these the poet "fetches . . . from the inmost Recesses of the Heart, describes them as they lurk there without Disguise, in all their genuine Conflicts" (p. 18). Trapp's sense of imitation, it ought to be noted, includes not only representations of action in plot but also the description of external objects and of passions, manners, and tempers of men. Certainly, a leading metaphor for the poet in the eighteenth century was that he was a "painter," a painter of both external and internal objects and events. Thomas Twining identified the representation of internal "objects" and "events" as one of the few genuinely imitative aspects of poetry, one that he distinguished from plot, the representation of an action.[49] The imitation of mind and manners in the "character" of Augustan satire is not the representation of an action; it is, rather, a painting—a portrait—of the mind. Using the metaphor of the poet-painter, Pope contrived the framework of "The

Characters of Women," the fiction of a portrait gallery in which each character is a painting representing the mind and manners of a given woman. In the poetry that he wrote before turning to the verse tale, Crabbe painted the passions; in his tales he traced the changing passions in a central action of the mind. The passions were, for Crabbe, outside the poet, objects of imitation, not sources of expression.

Passion is a constant in the eighteenth century, no matter who is speaking or what his views are. Trapp had said that passions must be fetched from deep recesses, imitated, painted, and Blair, that they must be expressed. Crabbe conceived of them as a process and this process as the action to be represented. Warton and later Bowles called certain kinds of poetry "genuine" because they conveyed the "natural" passions, and rejected other kinds of poetry because they rendered "artificial" passions, comprehended under the term *manners.*

For the eighteenth century there were two kinds of passions—natural and artificial—as there were two phases in their operations, one immediate and visible and the other permanent and invisible. Very simply, our passions are our internal motions, or agitations, or motives; they are the principles of our actions and the mark of our humanity. Ineradicable and necessary, they can be regulated by reason; without them we will stagnate.[50] Animal appetite and instinct supply the infant with the impulses necessary to activity and survival, but after infancy the passions, arising from appetite, begin to develop. These are our natural passions, common to all human beings, and they include the ancient pairs of hope and fear, love and hatred, desire and aversion. As our powers "extend their range . . . , as our reason strengthens, and our knowledge enlarges," a new kind of passion comes into being, for appetite and natural passions cannot keep the soul sufficiently employed. Thus "new desires, and artificial passions are by degrees produced," including avarice, vanity, and ambition; these we "never received from nature."[51] Accordingly, Bowles and

Warton denied the poetic validity of Pope's satires, which deal with the artificial passions appropriate to a particular society, whereas the passions of an Eloisa, the natural passions of love and grief, are innate in every human being. In the natural passions Bowles and Warton and others found what they believed were the essential attributes of humanity and of "genuine" poetry—general and natural forces. Crabbe, like Pope in his satiric vein, directed his attention to the artificial passions engendered by daily life. Like his age, Crabbe cherished the natural passions but in his verse tales told what happened to them in the "real" world.

Eighteenth-century theory of the passions held another important consequence for Crabbe and for narrative practice in general. I refer here to two distinct, though related, phases of the effects of passion, one external in its signs and the other internal in its consequences. The immediate effect of passion—anger, for example—is visible, powerful, transitory, turbulent, vehement; it may be likened to a storm, rising and subsiding swiftly. In the moment of its greatest intensity, the passion changes the whole demeanor of the person affected: "It changes the voice, the features, and the gesture. The external signs of passion have, in some cases, a great resemblance to those of madness; in others, to those of melancholy."[52] For many poets, especially the writers of pathetic tales, an elevation as high as madness or a depression as deep as melancholia was a temptation apparently irresistible, nor could they see any reason for resisting it; on the contrary: "It is from the natural signs of the passions and dispositions of the mind, that the human form derives its beauty; that painting, poetry, and music derive their expression; that eloquence derives its greatest force, and conversation its greatest charm" (p. 228). Admirable though these effects may be, there are internal dangers, for passion in its brief but irresistible moment of authority blinds the reason and falsifies reality, so that "*all deliberate Reasoning*" is difficult.[53] If a man is filled with the passion of resentment, internal and external reactions follow immediately: "His blood boils within him; his looks, his voice, and his gesture are changed; he can think of nothing but immediate revenge, and feels a strong impulse, without regard to consequences, to say and to do things which his cool reason cannot justify." Under the influence of a strong passion, he is a man possessed: "A man can hardly think of any thing else. . . . Like a magic lanthorn, it raises up spectres and apparitions that have no reality, and throws false colours upon every object," and the passion "often gives a violent impulse to the will, and makes a man do what he knows he shall repent as long as he lives."[54] The effect of a powerful passion was a splendid subject for poets, painters, critics, and for preachers, too, though for different reasons.

From the nature of man it was possible to derive an expressive literature that was exalted and exalting and that was designed to arouse our sympathy with declamation and gesture,[55] the immediate "audible" and "visible" effects of passion.[56] But there were other consequences of passion, permanent, invisible, protean; and it is these that matter most to Crabbe.

Passions create habits. Kames, in explaining how this comes about, cites first the "disposition" or temper of each man's mind, with its propensities that, in Kames's system at least, exist prior to any object or idea that might excite the passions. A man will be merry or morose, brash or cautious, depending upon his innate and individual disposition. This disposition, with the concurrence of external accidents, forms his character (3:394–95). The passion, excited by the desire for an object that seems pleasing or good, will agitate the mind and will ultimately modify it, for from the gratifications of passions arise habits: "To introduce a habit, frequency of acts is not alone sufficient: length of time is also necessary. . . . The circumstances then requisite to augment any pleasure and in the long run to form a habit, are weak, uniform acts, reiterated during a long course of time without any considerable interruption" (2:86–87). In the aggregate a man's habits will determine his "whole conduct, the entire system of his actions":

It is to habit he owes the greater part of his inclinations, of his desires, of his opinions, of his prejudices, of the ideas, true or false, he forms to himself of his welfare. In short, it is to habit, consecrated by time, that he owes those errors into which every thing strives to precipitate him. . . .

Man is so much modified by habit that it is frequently confounded with his nature.[57]

Godwin, who defined passion itself as "a permanent and habitual tendency toward a certain course of action . . . of the same general nature as avarice, or the love of fame," found that in "the history of every passion," passion produces habit and habit produces new passions; finally, habit survives even passion and pleasure.[58]

Blair, who as a literary critic admired the passions, feared and distrusted them as a preacher. In his sermons he discussed at length the dangers of gratified passions, for as virtue addresses itself to reason, so vice solicits the passions and "deprives sinners of the power of free choice, by bringing them under the dominion of passions and habits."[59] The passions "flatter us in their rise. But their beginnings are treacherous; their growth is imperceptible; and the evils which they carry . . . lie concealed, until their dominion is established."[60] Dominated by passion, a man cannot reflect, but when his "ardour is abated," he finds a "vicious habit rooted." The vehemence of a passion will necessarily diminish, but "when by long indulgence, it has established habits of gratification, the sinner's bondage becomes more confirmed and more miserable." Worst of all, the process is cumulative, for the sinner, solicited by his passions to vice, "must support one crime by means of another," and these, in turn, "render others necessary to which, against his inclination, he must submit. . . ." Consequently, "there arises a character of complicated vice; of luxury shooting forth into baseness, dishonesty, injustice, and perhaps cruelty":

It is thus that one favourite passion brings in a tribe of auxiliaries to complete the dominion of sin. Among all our corrupt passions there is a strong and intimate connection. When any one of them is adopted into our family, it never quits us until it has fathered upon us all its kindred.—By such means as these, by the violence of passions, by the power of habits, and by the connection of one vice with another, sin establishes that servitude over the will.[61]

Holbach the infidel agreed with Blair:

The first crime is always accompanied by more pangs of remorse than the second; this again, by more than the third, so on to those that follow. A first action is the commencement of a habit; those which succeed confirm it; by force of combating the obstacles that prevent the commission of criminal actions, man arrives at the power of vanquishing them with ease and facility. Thus he frequently becomes wicked from habit.[62]

The internal, or moral, consequence of the passions is not a series of heightened moments that create interesting external signs but, rather, an insidious process of long duration, in which a man's character is subtly transformed. It is a process to be analyzed and traced as it moves from almost imperceptible internal impulses to fixed, ineradicable consequences. This process is the action Crabbe represents in his verse tales. It is the center of his narrative art, an internal action in which passions are converted into habits and habits produce new passions. Particularly in *Tales in Verse,* he delineated the changing of a mind by means of the invisible impulses of passions gratified slowly one by one over a long period of time. The temporal scope of his tales is therefore often extensive, for he tried to encompass whole lifetimes in order to represent as comprehensively as possible the consequences of internal agitations and the transformations they worked. Crabbe and the novelists of the late eighteenth century appropriated this part of moral theory and adapted it to narrative. The mind's operations become the principle of narrative procedure.

3

THE PRECEPTIVE TALE

Informing the old-fashioned triad of satiric poetry—
minds, manners, and common life—with the vitality of
eighteenth-century moral theory, Crabbe fashioned this
material into short narrative poems. Was there anything in
eighteenth-century narrative theory that might have helped
him? Very little. Or in the practice of narrative verse? We
shall see. What is most obvious and perhaps most important
about eighteenth-century narrative theory is that there was
so little of it. Major critics and theorists, like Blair and
Kames, had little to say about the verse tale in particular or
narrative verse in general. The first is not surprising, the
second very much so. Of course, there are the inevitable
discussions of the epic with the related questions of celestial
machinery, pagan divinities, and the moral basis of the action, but the commentators rarely showed what might be
called a technical interest in the craft of narrative
poetry—with one significant exception, narrative description.

Not surprisingly, all writers on the subject of narrative
verse agreed that in any kind of narrative, great or small,
there must be a single action, an effectively contrived and

judiciously conducted fable, and well-conceived characters consistent in word and deed with themselves. Yet they were not concerned with such issues as the pace at which difficulties ought to accumulate or be resolved or the degree to which these should be emphasized or subordinated within the design of the whole. Blair, for example, gave only the most general advice about blocking out a narrative. Does a poet intend to speak in the third person? If so, he must begin at the beginning. Or does he plan to mix narrative and dramatic modes, letting his persons step forward at times to inform the reader of what has passed before? This method affords a number of advantages, particularly one: "It allows the poet . . . to open with some interesting situation of affairs, informing us afterwards of what had passed before that period; and gives the greater liberty of spreading out such parts of the subject as he is inclined to dwell upon in person, and of comprehending the rest within a short recital"[1]—a comprehensive description of the structure of the pathetic tale, the subject of the next chapter. As for coherence and pace, Anna Seward thought these were assured if a central character dominated the narrative; otherwise, the poem would be "a string of episodes rather than a series of events"[2]—an attractive solution, but, as Aristotle knew, not practical. As late as 1810, one critic, speaking of prose narrative, admitted that there were hardly any rules that would help: the taste and judgment of the narrator would be put to the test and his measures must be determined by his own best lights. Only example could guide.[3] All agreed that it was a difficult task, but no one cared to analyze the technical problems pertaining specifically to narrative verse. Critics enjoyed and praised successful narrations, but, except for the most general of inherited strictures, they were content to let the craft of the thing remain obscure and difficult.

Had all questions relative to the art of narrative been left in comparable obscurity, the silence about the structure and the shading of incident, character, and intrigue would be less noticeable. There was one question, however, that deeply interested the critics and that they discussed at length, the function of description in narrative verse. Josephine Miles has defined a century's tendency: "narrative declined and description gained in literary force."[4] Consider this passage from a letter Pope wrote in 1723:

> I could wish you tryd something in the descriptive way on any Subject you please, mixd with Vision & Moral. . . . I have long had an inclination to tell a Fairy tale; the more wild & exotic the better, therefore a *Vision,* which is confined to no rules of probability, will take in all the Variety & luxuriancy of Description you will. Provided there be an apparent moral to it. . . . And perhaps if the Scenes were taken from Real places that are known, in order to compliment particular Gardens & Buildings . . . it would add great beauty to the whole . . . If you did but, at leisure, form descriptions from Objects in nature itself which struck you most livelily, I would undertake to find a Tale that shoud bring em all together.[5]

As far as Pope is concerned, the verse tale is a means of holding descriptions together, and eighteenth-century literary theorists agreed. The theorists studied the art of description in detail, examining its sources in the writer's fancy and all its possible effects upon the reader. One can learn much about descriptive technique from reading Kames or Blair but little about the art of narrative. Why this concern with description to the neglect of every other technical consideration in narrative verse? The answer is obvious: If the story were not brought to the "eye" of the reader, it might as well not have been written at all, for it could neither please nor teach. Description became the essential element in effective narration, whereas structure, plot, and character were taken for granted.

A man cannot be moved by what he cannot see, and he will not think about what does not move him. For the eighteenth century, it was as simple as that. Narrative poetry, therefore, must be a "picture in words," first visualized in the poet's imagination and then in the reader's. If the poet failed to bring the circumstances of an event to his reader's eye, he failed in the first requirement of narrative.[6] His action might be single, his management of the intrigue judicious, and his characters natural, but unless the reader saw all this, his attention would flag. As Kames says:

> The force of language consists in raising complete images; which cannot be done till the reader, forgetting himself, be transported as by magic into the very place and time of the important action, and be converted, as it were, into a real spectator, beholding every thing that passes. In this view, the narrative in an epic poem ought to rival a picture in the liveliness and accuracy of its representations: no circumstance must be omitted that tends to make a complete image; because an imperfect image, as well as any other imperfect conception, is cold and uninteresting. (3:174–75)

Poet and reader were engaged in a mutual venture: the writer selected and forcefully represented the circumstances that would set the reader's fancy in action, and this faculty, supplied by memory, completed the image in the mind. In the eighteenth century, the reader was expected to do his share in image-making. That is why the twentieth-century reader often finds eighteenth-century poetry "vague" or "general," but it was not so to its contemporary reader. Again, Lord Kames:

> Shakespear says, "You may as well go about to turn the sun to ice by fanning in his face with a *peacock's* feather." The peacock's feather, not to mention the beauty of the object, completes the image. An accurate image cannot be formed of this fanciful operation, without conceiving a particular feather; and the mind is at some loss, when this is not specified in the description. (3:176)

The word *peacock* is the particular, specifying the kind of feather; the reader's fancy conceives a particular feather and presents it to the mind's eye. In the phrase *peacock's feather*, the twentieth-century reader sees a cold "general," but the fancy of the eighteenth-century reader created a warm particular. In fact, the poet was repeatedly cautioned against producing too minute a description that, in effect, would cheat the reader's fancy: *"the Mind of Man does not love to have too minute a Detail of Particulars; but takes a Pleasure in having Room for Imagination, and in forming a Judgment of what is not express'd, from what is."*[7] The most effective means of achieving "a sudden and strong impression" is, as Kames says, "some single circumstance happily selected" (3:180), which usually means the epithet, not Bysshe's epithet, intended to fill the line, but Blair's and Kames's, intended to fill eye, heart, and mind. These were the "strokes" of the verbal painting that the reader beheld. As Dodsley recognized, the epithet—"often a description in itself"—is especially useful in narration, "so much the more agreeable, as it the less retards us in our pursuit of the catastrophe."[8] Blair gives us a sense of what an eighteenth-century fancy could do with the epithet: Milton's "Deva's wizard stream" paints a whole scene, "presenting to the fancy all the romantic ideas, of a river flowing through a desolate country, with banks haunted by wizards and enchanters" (p. 556). Very clearly, the eighteenth-century reader, when he wished, took full advantage of the freedom offered his fancy and out of a single epithet produced a fully dimensioned scene.

Parnell, early in the century, concisely summarized the century's view. Bad narrations are "flat narrations"—no descriptions, no circumstances, no particulars—that "fail to profit while they fail to please"; good narrations are, very simply, descriptive:

> "Or if, with closer art, with sprightly mien,
> Scarce like herself, and more like Action seen,
> She bids their facts in images arise,
> And seem to pass before the reader's eyes
> ·

Here, as on circumstance narrations dwell,
And tell what moves, and hardly seem to tell."[9]

Heavy ornament, suitable for higher genres, is out of place
in the verse tale, and even metaphor should be used spar-
ingly, but description is a proper embellishment; indeed, it
is more than that: effective description makes effective narration possible.

Still, the definitive question for the short verse tale was its
usefulness. Preceptive and pathetic tales may be distinguished from one another by the answer to this question:
does a tale inculcate a precept or not? If it does not, it is a
pathetic tale, but if it does, it is a preceptive, or moral, tale
and, in Kames's words, enjoys

> an excellence peculiar to itself: for it not only improves
> the heart . . . but instructs the head by the moral it con-
> tains. For my part, I cannot imagine any entertainment
> more suited to a rational being, than a work thus happily
> illustrating some moral truth; where a number of persons
> of different characters are engaged in an important ac-
> tion, some retarding, others promoting the great catas-
> trophe. . . . A work of this kind, has our sympathy at
> command, and can put in motion the whole train of the
> social affections. We have at the same time great mental
> enjoyment, in perceiving every event and every subordi-
> nate incident connected with its proper cause. Our curios-
> ity is by turns excited and gratified; and our delight is
> consummated at the close, upon finding . . . that every
> circumstance down to the final catastrophe is natural, and
> that the whole in conjunction make a regular chain of
> causes and events. (3: 224)

John Newbery's *The Art of Poetry on a New Plan* offers a
compact definition of one kind of preceptive tale. Like
Kames, Newbery recognizes that the moral and the plot
must be integrated. For Newbery, the tale

implies nothing more than a relation of a simple action,

and therefore should not be embarassed with a multitude
of foreign circumstances, but may admit of such digres-
sions as arise naturally from the subject, and do not break
in upon, or obscure the main design. It should inculcate
some useful lesson, and be both interesting and perplexing, in order that it may excite and support the attention
of the reader; for great part of the pleasure or enter-
tainment which the mind receives from a well-written
Tale, will be found to arise from the suspense and anxiety
we are kept in; and which (as in the plot of a Tragedy or
Comedy) should not be removed till the end. Were the
whole scope and design, or, if I may so speak, the point of
the Tale first discovered, the reader would grow languid
and indifferent, and have nothing to attend to but the
diction and versification.[10]

What holds the reader is the adroit disposition of plot, the
interconnection of causes and effects unclear in their immediate relations and consequences, yet, when presented in
their entirety, coherent and instructive. This kind of tale
depends on incident to accomplish its purposes, its art being
the ingenious combination of incidents into a perplexing or
suspenseful but ultimately meaningful pattern. Stated or
implied, the precept in all tales of this kind is the active
principle (see Dodsley, pp. lix-lxiii). There is another version
of the preceptive tale, however, whose structure differs
from that of Newbery's preceptive and Kames's moral tale.
This is the progress tale, which will be discussed later in this
chapter.

Then there is the distinction between the tale and the
fable, one rigorously upheld in discussion and usually observed in practice: human beings are the agents in tales,
while fables are allegorical narrations in which nonhuman
agents represent human passions, virtues, vices.[11] The fable
is "decent"; the tale may or may not be. In eighteenth-
century England poets often felt a temptation, which they
seldom resisted, to overthrow a genre as edifying as the
preceptive tale: a gross story illustrates an irreproachable

maxim, and an ancient crew of old cuckolds, widows, young spouses, compliant serving maids fornicate frequently (or do not) or urinate copiously in the service of the higher virtues. And the range of precept is sweeping, moving from Parnell's noble conclusion,

> In this the right of Providence is laid;
> Its sacred majesty through all depends
> On using second means to work his ends,

to consolatory words drawn from a favorite topic at the end of William Whitehead's "The Dog. A Tale":

> "Small are the ills we now endure,
> Those tumours, sir, admit a cure.
> But, had I done as you directed,
> Whose forehead then had been affected?
> Had captain Wilkins been forbidden,
> Ah master, who had then been ridden?"

—and then to Burns's

> When'er to drink you are inclin'd,
> Or cutty-sarks run in your mind,
> Think, ye may buy the joys o'er dear,
> Remember Tam o' Shanter's mare,

and on to the worthy Hannah More's

> 'Tis self-denying moderation
> Gains the Great Father's approbation.[12]

Among the many verse tales at the disposal of the eighteenth-century anthologist, Newbery selected two as particularly noteworthy, Thomas Parnell's serious and "moral" tale, "The Hermit," and John Gay's "An Apparition," indecent but exemplary. These two poems indicate the range of the preceptive tale, how readily it serves the purposes of moralizing or of indecency at the same time that it invariably fulfills its generic purpose, the drawing of a perplexed or suspended reader toward the revelation of a governing precept.

"The Hermit" was the most highly esteemed preceptive tale published during the eighteenth century. One critic praised it for its "great perspicuity and preciseness";[13] Blair discovered its value in his own bias: it was a "beautiful descriptive narration" affording "pieces of very fine painting, touched with a light and delicate pencil, overcharged with no superfluous colouring, and conveying to us a lively idea of the objects" (p. 551). Newbery, of course, cited it as a model of its kind (2: 235). "The Hermit" is indeed impeccable miniature painting, for in this tale Parnell and his reviser Pope did what Parnell had advised others to do in the "Essay on the Different Styles of Poetry." The treatment of the story is comprehensively and consistently descriptive, bringing to the reader's eye the minds of the characters, the scenes through which they move, and the actions they perform. The perplexities created for the reader—and for the central character as well—arise from, lead into, and are resolved in the culminating incident by the very precept that it is the business of the tale to illustrate.

The action—learning the ways of Providence—is represented in six clearly defined incidents. A hermit, journeying through the world in order to resolve his doubts about Providence, meets a young man who, in the course of three days and four incidents, performs four inexplicable acts: a theft from a generous man, a gift to a miser, and two gratuitous murders. In the principal incident the stranger is suddenly transformed into an angel, who speaks the precept justifying God's mysterious ways to man. The growing perplexity of hermit and reader that each bewildering incident has fostered is dissolved as the scope and plan of the whole tale and the whole universe are revealed.

Incident, the basic unit of structure in this tale, is blocked out according to a uniform pattern. Time of day and place provide its setting, and the "mind"—the native disposition and ruling passion—of each of the men the hermit encounters is illustrated in setting and gesture. Time, place, mind, act, and response are brought by descriptive circumstances to the reader's eye, and all are subordinated to the design and conduct of the whole. What is especially important is the balance that Parnell achieves among these elements of narrative, the harmony produced by his adherence to economy as a principle of narration and style.

In each incident circumstances of the time of day or the weather frame the action and at the same time provide the occasion for the incident:

> Now sunk the Sun; the closing hour of day
> Came onward, mantled o'er with sober grey;
> Nature in silence bid the world repose;
> When near the road a stately palace rose.
>
> (p. 366)

Time also generates incident, for it requires that the travelers stop at a given place; the incident itself is governed by the mind of the person the hermit meets, as in this passage, where the moral qualities of a character are given their visual equivalents in a landscape:

> Warn'd by the signs, the wand'ring pair retreat,
> To seek for shelter at a neighbouring seat.
> 'Twas built with turrets, on a rising ground,
> And strong, and large, and unimprov'd around;
> Its owner's temper, timorous and severe,
> Unkind and griping, caus'd a desert there.
>
> (p. 366)

The events within the hermit's mind are also represented in descriptive circumstances, with descriptive ornament explaining, defining, and contributing to the advance of the action. The perturbations of the hermit's mind are painted in a simile:

> But if a stone the gentle sea divide,
> Swift ruffling circles curl on every side,
> And glimmering fragments of a broken Sun,
> Banks, trees, and skies, in thick disorder run.

(p. 366)

On another disquieting occasion, the agitations of the mind are rendered by their external signs:

> He stop'd with silence, walk'd with trembling heart,
> And much he wish'd, but durst not ask to part:
> Murmuring he lifts his eyes, and thinks it hard,
> That generous actions meet a base reward.

and are brought to the reader's eye in a simile at once ornamental and explanatory:

> As one who spies a serpent in his way,
> Glistening and basking in the summer ray,
> Disorder'd stops to shun the danger near,
> Then walks with faintness on, and looks with fear.

(p. 366)

The agitations of a bewildered mind—fear, anger, and wonder—define the progressive action of the tale; the question "what does all this mean?" enforces continuity. A seemingly irrational interconnection of incidents and of deserts and rewards works for the reader's and hermit's growing perplexity, until at last, before their eyes, the mysterious and criminal youth becomes an angel who pronounces the all-explaining precept: "His youthful face grew more serenely sweet; / His robe turn'd white, and flow'd upon his feet" (p. 367).

To use Dodsley's terms, description is "included in the action" (p. lxxvi) of "The Hermit," performing a number of functions essential to plot. The minds and acts of the characters and the scenes in which they move exist in a state of representational balance, mutually reinforcing one another, while the reader, the interested spectator, beholds the story in its entirety. He sees but does not participate in what is happening. This nice sense of proportion did not hold throughout the century. In Somerville's verse tale, "The Officious Messenger," action is sacrificed to minute description; in another, Whitehead's "The Dog," all is subordinated to rapidity of narration. In Gay's "An Apparition" the beginning of an important change in narrative technique is apparent, one requiring that the reader participate in the incidents, not merely behold them.

The reader of "The Hermit" asks, "What is the meaning of all this?" Gay, however, suspends both his narrative and his reader by delaying the onset of the next turn of events. The difference between perplexity and suspense is slight, but it is nonetheless real. Perplexity arises when one cannot perceive the relation of one thing to another; suspense, when one is uncertain about what will happen next, and suspense is intensified by delay. Gay and Parnell therefore use different methods of presentation in order to accommodate their different means of creating interest and of holding attention. Gay employs description throughout his tale as a way, first, of securing delay and, second, of forcing the reader to become a vicarious participant in the events.

The action of "An Apparition" is the destruction of unnatural hopes by natural facts. A traveler, lost in a storm, happens upon an inn, where, after being lodged in the haunted room, he is visited by a ghost who leads him to buried treasure and then suddenly disappears just as the traveler awakens from his dream of treasure to discover that he has wet the bed. The precept follows: "What is the statesman's vast ambitious scheme, / But a short vision, and a golden dream?" (ll. 139–40).[14] In Gay's tale, incident is not the clear-cut unit of structure that it is in "The Hermit"; instead, setting is aggrandized at the expense of the other parts of the narrative, for "An Apparition" is a Gothic tale, and its existence suggests that by 1720 the rudiments of this mode were sufficiently established to permit a burlesque.

There is only one step between being a spectator and a participant; Gay's tale begins to take that step, and little more than a shifting of perspectives is needed to effect a change in the principle of composition. Parnell painted the landscape of sky and earth and brought setting and character to the eye—his scenery is illustrative, distinct, definable. The reader sees the incidents taking place in a larger, though relevant, setting; but in "An Apparition" the reader sees usually only what the hero sees, and both hero and reader, by the nature of the subject and the methods employed in treating it, are moved toward the same end, allegedly a good scare. "The Hermit" opens with a brief exposition summarizing the hermit's way of life, his habits, his thoughts; Gay's "dreadful tale" begins:

> Where Arden's forest spreads its limits wide,
> Whose branching paths the doubtful road divide,
> A traveller took his solitary way,
> When low beneath the hills was sunk the day.
>
> (ll. 29–32)

Place and time are carefully specified, but character is not. The reader does not know what the traveler's life has been, what worries him, or even what sends him on his journey; unlike the hermit, he seems to have no moral existence, no mind—no native disposition and no ruling passion. All one knows is that he is solitary and caught in a storm:

> And now the skies with gathering darkness lour,
> The branches rustle with the threaten'd shower;
> With sudden blasts the forest murmurs loud,
> Indented lightnings cleave the sable cloud,
> Thunder on thunder breaks, the tempest roars,
> And Heaven discharges all its watery stores.

The wandering traveller shelter seeks in vain,
And shrinks and shivers with the beating rain.

(ll. 33–40)

A storm in "The Hermit" occurs in a changing landscape, in which ornamental clouds obscure a regularly recurring sun (it has made its circuit two times already in the poem), in which livestock move, and in which turrets and fields illustrate a certain temper of mind:

While thus they pass, the Sun his glory shrouds,
The changing skies hang out their sable clouds;
A sound in air presag'd approaching rain,
And beasts to covert scud across the plain.
Warn'd by the signs the wandering pair retreat.

(p. 366)

Gay's storm is intended to close in not only on the hero but also on the reader, whereas Parnell's storm is "composed" around the figures in the poem: "Fierce rising gusts with sudden fury blew; / . . . And o'er their heads loud rolling thunders ran." The reader can see only the storm in Gay's tale, not the picture of travelers in a storm. I exaggerate an effect here in order to point to a tendency, a discernibly Gothic one. There is, moreover, a degree of specificity in "An Apparition" that is missing in "The Hermit":

On his steed's neck the slacken'd bridle lay,
Who chose with cautious step th' uncertain way;
And now he checks the rein, and halts to hear
If any noise foretold a village near.

(ll. 33–36)

These lines do not serve to advance the action; rather, they suspend and delay it. To delay in narrative is to amplify or to digress. Gay chose to amplify here, and although this tale, when compared to later eighteenth-century narratives, seems very concise, it does not seem so when set beside

"The Hermit." In the following passage one can see how Gay's method again diverges from Parnell's:

> At length from far a stream of light he sees
> Extends its level ray between the trees;
> Thither he speeds, and as he nearer came
> Joyful he knew the lamp's domestic flame
> That trembled through the window; cross the way
> Darts forth the barking cur, and stands at bay.
>
> (ll. 45–50)

The details of the object seen, not the temper of mind seeing it, receive the poet's attention. Gay simulates the experience of one approaching an isolated dwelling; from a distance, the lamp is perceived in general terms as domestic, but as the rider approaches the house, he sees the flame with increasing specificity until the barking dog leaps forward and breaks off this imitation of experience. "Do you not," Joseph Warton asked the reader of Pope's "Epistle to Bathurst," "*actually* find yourself in the middle court of this forlorn and solitary mansion . . . ? And do you not hear the dog that is going to assault you?"[15] Characters in Gay's tale are subordinated to—rather, absorbed by—the setting: "Swift at the gate the ready landlord stands; / With frequent cringe he bows, and begs excuse" (ll. 60–61). More than a ghost and a gust of wind is needed to make a Gothic tale; as Sir Walter Scott observed of Ann Radcliffe's fiction, there must be an essential reduction of "mind" and a corresponding amplification of setting. "The force . . . of the production, lies in the delineation of external incident, while the characters of the agents, like the figures in many landscapes, are entirely subordinate to the scenes in which they are placed; and are only distinguished by such outlines as make them seem appropriate to the rocks and trees, which have been the artist's principal objects."[16] The beauty of Gay's landlord is that he has no mind: the gestures make the picture and signify little. In this tale one finds a concern with the pictorial for its own sake; the unfolding of the scene rather than the plot holds "An Apparition" together.

Nearly a century intervened between the composition of "The Hermit" and "An Apparition" and the publication in 1812 of Crabbe's tale "The Lover's Journey" (*Tales in Verse*). Clearly, much had happened to narrative during this interval. Crabbe, reducing "The Lover's Journey" to a direct collision between the mind of the central character and the reality that he persistently misreads, dwells upon the minutiae of thought, feeling, and external object. In order to carry out these purposes, he virtually discards plot, whereas Gay only diminished it and Parnell consummately organized it. The balanced relations of action, plot, character, and description seem now to belong far in the past; Crabbe is working with problems and possibilities that are alien, even hostile, to Parnell's narrative balance. Nonetheless, "The Lover's Journey" has its precept or—if you prefer—its thesis:

> It is the soul that sees; the outward eyes
> Present the object, but the mind descries;
> And thence delight, disgust, or cool indiff'rence rise.[17]

(ll. 1–3)

The story demonstrates the validity of this statement. A cheerful young man goes to visit the girl he loves but learns that she is visiting friends a short distance away. Angrily, he goes there, sees her, is reconciled, and returns home by the same road that he came, noticing nothing, lost as he is in thoughts of her. It is a single incident broken into three phases of the mind, arousing neither perplexity nor suspense, but offering instead as its center of interest the relation of subject and object.

Crabbe organizes his narrative by means of contrast: he contrasts states of mind as well as the reality of the scene with the mind's false assessment of it; description renders reality and declamation presents the views of the passion-dominated mind. Description is juxtaposed with declamation, reality with seeming. In Parnell's tale the reader sees the hermit's external and internal responses; in Gay's tale he usually sees only what the traveler sees; but in Crabbe's tale he sees the "real" world and a false assessment of it, and the contrast of the two is the essence of the tale. What creates the unity of "The Lover's Journey" is not that all incidents lead toward a turn and a lesson, but simply that the same mind, various as its responses may be, is at work from the beginning to the end of the tale.

During the first—the happy—part of the journey, the young man passes through a bleak, impoverished landscape:

> He saw some scatter'd hovels; turf was piled
> In square brown stacks; a prospect bleak and wild!
> A mill, indeed, was in the centre found,
> With short sear herbage withering all around;
> A smith's black shed opposed a wright's long shop,
> And join'd an inn where humble travellers stop.
>
> (ll. 68–73)

Animated by hope and joy, the hero sees only what he feels: "'Ay, this is Nature,' said the gentle 'squire; / 'This ease, peace, pleasure—who would not admire?' " (ll. 74–75). In Gay's tale the settlement would have been the setting for the action; in Parnell's, matters would have been so represented that the reader would know the moral character of the owner. In both poems, for one reason or another, the scene would have been carefully adjusted to the telling of the tale. In Crabbe's tale, however, there is hardly any plot operating and therefore there is no perplexity or suspense. The reader reads on, not because the narrative is working toward an unforeseen end, but simply because he is engaged in a minute-by-minute process of observing a mind deceiving itself about what is before it. In "The Lover's Journey" place after place and object after object are subjected to the same inaccurate reading. The reader himself is not expected to say, "What can this mean?" or "Now, what will happen?" but, rather, "How true. That is exactly the way it is."

Crabbe, moreover, insists on bringing "reality" to the page by painting "things as they are" in descriptions that earlier poets would have regarded as entirely too labored and tedious; he paints in the manner of the "low" Dutch school, not in the manner of Claude. At one moment in his journey the hero encounters a group of gypsies; he does not see the misery of these people, but the reader does. To the exclusion of other interests, Crabbe enforces the actuality of his subject and the complexity of the mind:

> On ragged rug, just borrow'd from the bed,
> And by the hand of coarse indulgence fed,
> In dirty patchwork negligently dress'd,
> Reclin'd the wife, an infant at her breast;
> In her wild face some touch of grace remain'd,
> Of vigour palsied and of beauty stain'd;
> Her blood-shot eyes on her unheeding mate
> Were wrathful turn'd, and seem'd her wants to state,
> Cursing his tardy aid.
>
> (ll. 166–74)

Compare this passage to a single line from "The Hermit": "Wild, sparkling rage inflames the father's eyes. . . ." The conciseness of Parnell's description simplifies the mind, whereas Crabbe's description is copious—"tedious"—because his description must register the fine shades of the actuality of the woman's suffering. He has sought to convey the complexity of a mind in a single instant of its working and to imply in that instant the whole of its history. The bloodshot eyes, the wrathful glance, and the unexpressed wish, like the gypsy woman herself, contribute nothing to the plot of "The Lover's Journey." They are included because they are *real*. In his determination to render things as they are, Crabbe sacrifices narrative continuity to dwell upon the details of a familiar scene. The details themselves acquire force and cannot be subordinated to any controlling plan, insisting, as they do, on their own actuality at the expense of narrative unity. Amplification isolates and strengthens the part while it fragments the whole. The traditional narrative intention that one incident lead into another and that all cohere as parts of a complete action is scarcely working in "The Lover's Journey." No plot mediates between mind and reality, only the falsifying passions. Scene, passion, and mind, elements with which Parnell creates a rather wonderful narrative equilibrium, are still to be found in Crabbe's tale, but with a new and disproportionate distribution of relative weights, for in "The Lover's Journey" these terms have broken away from virtually every control but the theory of the mind that the tale is intended to illustrate.

It would be a mistake, nevertheless, to conclude that Crabbe's tales bear no relation at all to the work of his preceptive predecessors. For one thing, in *Tales in Verse*, only seven out of the twenty-one tales neither begin nor end preceptively, and each exception enforces an implied moral with a powerful example. Still, one can remove the precept from Crabbe's tales and the integrity of his narratives will remain, whereas the precept cannot be removed from Gay's or Parnell's tales without making the whole narrative meaningless. The precept was not the end toward which Crabbe directed his narratives.[18]

There is, moreover, another kind of preceptive tale, the progress, which bears an important relation to Crabbe's work. The progress itself assumed many different forms during the eighteenth century; it is found in allegory, ode, georgic, and verse tale as well as in the visual arts. Karl Kroeber, apparently with Hogarth's progresses in mind, has said that "the basic pattern of all Crabbe's narratives . . . is that of the Progress, which enumerates in defined stages the course of punishments attendant upon a particular vice." Kroeber's definition of the progress is too narrow, even for Hogarth; there is, after all, the virtuous apprentice as well as the idle one, nor can all of Crabbe's narratives be so characterized, although many can be. To Kroeber, a proponent of organic art, the progress is a "mechanical form" that is "imposed upon the individual's biography" and that "encourages the presentation of simplified characterizations."[19] He underestimates Crabbe's art in this respect. Other scholars have been more specific, notably Oliver Sigworth,[20] who has pointed to the similarity existing between Crabbe's tales and Swift's "Phillis, Or, the Progress of Love," a tetrameter tale that offers no explicit precept but whose whole scope and design constitute a warning against romantic marriages: Phillis progresses from vain coquette to runaway bride to whore and, finally, to landlady of an inn.

The progress tale is the edifying narrative that traces a history—of a fop, a wit, a miser, a passion—and from it the reader may either gather the useful lesson by inference or read it directly in a precept. In the tale Newbery described, the intricacies of the plot are important and incident is rendered fully; in the progress tale, it is a process, not the involutions of story, that governs the telling of the tale. The tendency in the progress tale is to summarize a number of incidents; in Newbery's tale, to emphasize and to particularize incident. In the first, the reader recognizes the general truth of the progress; in the second, he is perplexed or held in suspense about the tale's meaning or outcome. Goldsmith's "The Double Transformation," for example, is the story of a wife who, presuming too much on her beauty, progressively becomes more impudent and slatternly until the loss of beauty reverses the process and she moves back to humility and neatness. Pope's "Sir Balaam" presents a man's gradual progress from virtue to vice and damnation, and Swift's "Progress of a Marriage" recounts an aging husband's progress toward death in his attempt to get an heir from his young wife.

As a narrative kind, then, the progress is essentially concerned with process, with the chain of causes and effects

at carry a passion or person from a beginning to a logical
onclusion. Accordingly, it is rendered *seriatim*, a summary
f events saved from flatness by the rapidity of its narration
nd its quick, particularizing strokes, as in Swift's "Phillis":

> But what Adventures more befel 'um,
> The Muse has now no time to tell 'um.
> How Jonny wheadled, threatned, fawnd,
> Till Phillis all her Trinkets pawn'd:
> How oft she broke her marriage Vows
> In kindness to maintain her Spouse.
> 　　　　　　　　　　　　(ll. 85–90)[21]

n its purest form, the progress assigns equal compositional
alue to each event in the series; none is subordinated to or
levated above another, and none is sufficiently defined so
s to become a discrete incident in itself. Thomas Warton's
The Progress of Discontent" is an instance of this kind of
rogress. There is no principal incident on which every-
ning turns or toward which everything tends. The hero is
iscontented as a student and wishes he were a fellow; he
ecomes a fellow and wishes he had a parish and a wife; he
btains both and wishes he were back in college. That is the
tory, that is the structure of Warton's progress. The struc-
ure of Swift's "Phillis" differs from that of Warton's "Dis-
ontent." The first ten lines describe Phillis's character; the
ext fifty-four present the principal incident—her elope-
nent with John the butler; and the last twenty-two lines
race the events that follow the marriage. The structure is
nlike that of Warton's progress, but both employ the same
epresentational technique, the rapid narration of events in
series, which I shall call, for the sake of convenience,
quasi incidents":

> The Mother scream'd, the Father chid,
> Where can this idle Wench be hid?
> No news of Phil. The Bridegroom came,
> And thought his Bride had sculk't for shame.
> 　　　　　　　　　　　　(ll. 27–30)

Crabbe's "William Bailey," in *Tales of the Hall,* begii
where Swift's tale ends, with William Bailey and his wi
serving as proprietors of an inn. The story of how th
came to be there is told retrospectively, and the min
figure in "Phillis," the disappointed bridegroom, is the he
of Crabbe's tale. "William Bailey" is the story of William
mind; the virtuous integrity of his native disposition is a
fected but never corrupted by love for a girl who abandoi
him to run away with a nobleman's son. The principal inc
dent toward which all this tends is the accidental meeting
William and the middle-aged woman whom he once love
They meet, marry at last, and set up together as innkeeper
Swift's tale has one hundred lines; Crabbe's has 731 line
What accounts for this remarkable difference in lengtl
First, Crabbe is interested in what does not at all concer
Swift, the minutiae of William Bailey's mental history as l
moves from youth to middle age. Second, where Swi
summarizes, Crabbe presents; that is, he creates inciden
Swift's

> The Mother scream'd, the Father chid,
> Where can this idle Wench be hid?
>
> (ll. 27–2&

becomes in Crabbe's tale

> "Think! yes, my lord! but thinking drives me mad—
> "Give me my child!—Where is she to be had?
> "I'm old and poor, but I with both can feel,
> "And so shall he that could a daughter steal!
> . . . .
> "Old if I am, could I the robber meet
> "I'd lay his breathless body at my feet—
> "Was that a smile, my lord? think you your boy
> "Will both the father and the child destroy?"
> My lord replied— "I'm sorry, from my soul!
> "But boys are boys, and there is no control."—
> . . . .

"Will your son marry?"—"Marry!" said my lord,
"Your daughter?—marry—no, upon my word!"
(ll. 431–446, *passim*)[22]

Swift's purpose is to summarize Phillis's progress toward the
Blue Boar Inn as rapidly as possible, but Crabbe pauses to
elaborate for pathetic effect. Swift has summarized a
number of incidents; Crabbe has represented an incident,
and insofar as fully rendered incident appears, the progress
disappears. In Crabbe's tales, incident rises out of a progress, the pathetic consequence of an ethical process. For
Crabbe, the progress was useful not as a genre but as a
narrative method, one especially congenial to him, because,
like the writers of the progress, he wished to represent a
process in its entirety. Yet, as Sigworth has said, one of the
most important differences between Crabbe's work and a
poem like Swift's "Phillis" is that Crabbe wished to create
sympathy for his characters (pp. 117–18), and that, as we
shall see, requires a technique and a structure alien to the
progress.

William Whitehead's tale "Variety," like many of the tales
in Crabbe's *Tales in Verse,* is a progress consisting of quasi-
incidents culminating in a principal incident in which
the characters express their feelings about the consequences of this progress. In Whitehead's poem a young husband and wife progress from rural innocence to urban dissipation in a search for variety:

> For rural visits, now and then,
> Are right, as men must live with men.
> Then cousin Jenny, fresh from town,
>   A new recruit, a dear delight!
> Made many a heavy hour go down,
>   At morn, at noon, at eve, at night;
> Sure they could hear her jokes for ever,
> She was so sprightly and so clever!
>   Yet neighbours were not quite the thing;
> What joy, alas! could converse bring

> With awkward creatures bred at home—
> The dog grew dull, or troublesome.
> The cat had spoil'd the kitten's merit,
> And with her youth, had lost her spirit.
> And jokes repeated o'er and o'er,
> Had quite exhausted Jenny's store.
>
> (p. 235)[23]

As the search for variety continues, the marriage progressively disintegrates until finally, in the principal incident, husband and wife confront each other and the truth, as the poem's method shifts from summary to the dialogue and "descriptive narration" of fully rendered incident:

> At last they met, by his desire,
> A-*tête-à-tête* across the fire;
> Look'd in each other's face awhile,
> With half a tear, and half a smile.
> . . . .
> Silence is eloquence, 'tis said.
> Both wish'd to speak, both hung the head.
> At length it burst.—" 'Tis time," he cries,
> "When tir'd of folly, to be wise.
> "Are you too tir'd?"—then check'd a groan.
> She wept consent, and he went on.
>
> (p. 236)

Crabbe's intention in a comparable tale is far more complex than Whitehead's, because the passions and minds he represents are more complex than those in Whitehead's tale. In " 'Squire Thomas; Or, the Precipitate Choice," plot is more important than it is in "The Lover's Journey," but, even so, Crabbe's interest here is not in the involutions of a plot but of a mind. A series of quasi-incidents culminating in two fully rendered incidents, including the principal incident, gives the tale its particular shape.

> 'Squire Thomas flatter'd long a wealthy aunt,
> Who left him all that she could give or grant:

Ten years he tried, with all his craft and skill,
To fix the sovereign lady's varying will;
Ten years enduring at her board to sit,
He meekly listened to her tales and wit;
He took the meanest office man can take,
And his aunt's vices for her money's sake.
By many a threat'ning hint she waked his fear,
And he was pain'd to see a rival near;
Yet all the taunts of her contemptuous pride
He bore, nor found his grov'ling spirit tried.

(ll. 1–12)[24]

After his patient greed has won him his fortune, the squire's avarice gives way to pride; from the demands of pride comes love, and at the conclusion of the tale, when love is disappointed, avarice, resumes its old sway, greater now even than hatred. The squire, in his pride, has been trapped in a cold, mean, loveless marriage, arranged by relatives who had been denied their share of the aunt's fortune. In the principal incident his wife tells him the truth, offers to divide the money as the price of a separation, and to go her way in peace. In spite of his hatred of his wife, he cannot part with the money, and husband and wife must spend the rest of their lives at war. Crabbe brings the conflicting and fluctuating passions within Squire Thomas's mind to the eye of the reader in the principal incident. While fear and resentment contend, avarice resumes its habitual authority:

Our hero trembling heard—he sat—he rose—
Nor could his motions nor his mind compose;
He paced the room—and, stalking to her side,
Gazed on the face of his undaunted bride;
And nothing there but scorn and calm aversion spied.
He would have vengeance, yet he fear'd the law:
Her friends would threaten, and their power he saw;
"Then let her go;" but oh! a mighty sum
Would that demand, since he had let her come.

(ll. 335–43)

" 'Squire Thomas," like "The Lover's Journey," is a tale in which an internal process constitutes the action of the tale and its central interest. Unlike Parnell, Crabbe does not build his narrative out of separate, descriptively rendered and integrally related incidents, nor does he concentrate on a continuous development of scene, as does Gay. In "The Hermit" and "An Apparition" the internal action of the characters is subordinated to the unfolding of the story, and their internal history, insofar as they may be said to have one, exists primarily in relation to the telling of the tale; but in Crabbe's work the tale exists for the sake of the internal events that constitute a process. In his tales external reality is powerfully present in description, but the primary purpose of his description is to reveal how certain passions are operating on a particular disposition of mind. And so with the incidents that Crabbe contrives: these too are designed to show how particular passions work on a particular kind of mind under the pressures of a decisive moment, in itself the consequence of a long train of causes and effects, of passions and habits.

In delineating this process, Crabbe found the progress a necessary method—it was the one thing that the preceptive tradition offered him that he could use, and in some tales he used it supremely well. His narratives flag and grow awkward, not when he is delineating the progress of his characters from passion to habit and from old habit to new passions, but when he comes to the principal incident, when declamation is required. Swift and Whitehead, like other narrators of the progress tale, sacrificed the minutiae of the mind's operations in order to concentrate on rapidity of narration, but Crabbe was interested primarily in tracing the subtle motions of a mind moving toward a self-set trap. It is the complexity of his subject and the microscopic intensity of his examination that distinguish his tales from theirs.

Eighteenth-century narrative theory had little to teach Crabbe or any other poet about the art of narrative verse, except its lessons in description, and Crabbe had learned those long before he began writing tales. Like his colleagues, he was thrown back upon the narratives of his predecessors and contemporaries—these were the only guides to the craft available to him. What is interesting about Crabbe's relation to Newbery's preceptive tale is how little he cared to learn from it. In contrast to all that Parnell could have taught him in the way of balanced and beautiful narrative, he chose the progress and chose to make that progress lengthy, detailed—to deprive it of its chief virtue, its conciseness, and to break it up with incidents—all this because his profound interest in the motions of the mind dominated his entire narrative art and because he compelled himself to work for pathetic effects.

4

THE PATHETIC TALE

The pathetic tale is a curious mixture of elegiac personal intensity and tragic declamation within a loose narrative frame. It is to be distinguished from the Ovidian narrative, popular around the turn of the seventeenth century, by its emphasis on declamation rather than narrative. More significantly, since it has "no tendency beyond moving the passions,"[1] its structure is radically different from that of the preceptive tale. Although a pathetic tale does not instruct, ideally it ought to make its reader a better person; as Kames said, by working upon the reader's sympathy, the pathetic tale improves his heart, for in rejoicing and grieving on behalf of virtue, he learns to love the good and hate the wicked (3: 225). However, the pleasure derived from reading about imaginary sufferings raised problems both moral and aesthetic for the eighteenth century. Is it, as some thought, that we sympathize with fictional characters in imaginary distress because we fearfully recognize that such things could happen to us; is not our pleasure in pathetic compositions of all kinds that of titillated self-interest soothed by the rational certainty that, in truth, these are not our sufferings? Or is it, as another group thought, pure, disinterested benevolence that encourages us to suffer with fictive beings, and is not the aftermath of all this indulgence in good feeling very much like the gratification that follows a good deed, our own self-approbation? The first view, which is Samuel Johnson's, made the benevolists uneasy; it suggested that there is no escape from our selfishness, not even in our sympathy. For the honor of humankind, they repudiated this "Hobbesian" view of art and man.[2] The writers of pathetic tales, it may be said, shared the second view, and, in order to insure their reader's pleasure, produced narratives that are elevated above the actualities of common life. After reading a pathetic tale, the responsive eighteenth-century reader, who successively felt the dismay and joys of the characters, enjoyed a sense of his own goodness, unimpeded by any real asperities in the subject.

The pathetic tale proved to be a most adaptable genre. It could be extended to the verse novel, or a drama could be converted into a pathetic tale. Bishop Percy gave it the trappings of a ballad, just as Prior had earlier adapted the ballad to it. It could deal with modest rural worth or aristocratic turmoil; it could be thrust into the present or moved back into the past, and historical figures as well as imaginary beings peopled its scenes. In the pathetic tale the action is delineated in an exchange of declamations; the plot itself consists of those events which have taken place before the opening of the tale, and the solution of present problems, the consequence of those off-stage events, constitutes the brief action of the tale. The writer of this kind of narrative was not interested in representing a concatenation of incidents or a series of events, but, rather, in representing a discovery and its attendant reversal of fortune. The pathetic tale may be described as *peripeteia in medias res*. Using the declamation as the basic unit of structure, the pathetic narrator attended to events and emotions at their moment of crisis. Of necessity, his scope was limited, for passion is brief. The passions themselves

rouze the dormant power of the soul. They are even
found to exalt them. They often raise a man above himself. . . . He is inspired with more lofty sentiments, and
endowed with more persuasive utterance, than he posses-
ses at any other time. Passions are the active forces of the
soul.[3]

Exalted by their emotions, the characters in pathetic tales
express themselves in a correspondingly exalted style, or-
namented with questions, exclamations, hyperboles,
metaphors, similes, comparisons, personifications, and
apostrophes—the passionate figures of speech, invariable
signs of the passion-inflamed imagination. The writer of the
pathetic tale sought to create a style as elevated as he supposed the passions elevating and, in exploring the literary
possibilities of heightened states of being, forged an improbable eloquence.

Nevertheless, as far as the eighteenth century was concerned, the pathetic tale was a pleasing venture; its declamatory mode allowed the reader to delight in "seeing"
and "hearing" the gathering and culminating passions of
the vocal and gesticulating characters.[4] The popularity of
Prior's "Henry and Emma," which continued from the first
decade of the century to the last, is a case in point; this
pathetic tale was not merely admired; it was loved, and
loved by an audience that included adolescent girls,
Cowper, Shenstone, and Percy.[5] If for a time a quieter style
seemed to be making some headway in the pathetic tale,
notably in certain literary ballads, this "pathetic simplicity,"
succumbed soon, as if by contagion, to more excited and
elevated language. Yet, the pathetic tale did not survive its
century or the literary and psychological assumptions on
which it rested, nor does an understanding of those assumptions revivify this once lively genre. It is dead now
because it was once, all too often, mere rant. Pope, early in
the century, recognized that stylistic confusion was overtaking both narrative and dramatic poetry. As he saw it, it was
his "duty" in his translation of Homer

to observe a certain mediocrity of Style, agreeable to Conversation and Dialogue, which is called the Narrative, and ought to be low, being put into the mouths of persons not of the highest condition, or of a person acting in the disguise of a poor Wanderer, & speaking in that character of consequence. . . . Nothing is so ridiculous as the lofty or poetical style in such parts, which yet many Poets (& no very mean ones) are often guilty of, especially in our modern Tragedy, where one continued Sameness of Diction runs thro' all their Characters. . . . In like manner our modern Poets preserve a painful Equality of Fustian, throughout their whole Epic or Tragic works. . . . To write thus upon low subjects is really the true Sublime of Ridicule . . . : It leaves no distinction between the Language of Gods, which is when the Muse or the Gods speak, and that of men, in the Conversation & Dialogues.[6]

The pathetic narrator chose to speak the language of gods and ignore the language of men.

Although it did not instruct, the pathetic tale was intended to be more "serious" than the preceptive tale. It was "high"—it elevated, idealized, and simplified both characters and story. Prior, Young, Thomson, Shenstone, Mallet, Percy, Goldsmith, Seward, Scott, Bloomfield, and Montgomery,[7] with variations in their intentions and applications, produced pathetic tales. As the century went on, the pathetic narrators became even more solemn about their work: the less distinguished the poet, the more he seemed to think he was doing. During the years that Crabbe was learning his art, this was the dominant narrative kind in verse. It was the *serious* verse tale, while the preceptive tale seems to have lost its moral authority as time passed; interestingly enough, during the later decades of the eighteenth century, the pathetic tale became more "moral." As the distinctions between pathos and ethos broke down, the later pathetic narrators put moral sentiments of the most elevated kind in the mouths of their characters; earlier there were none of these. Thomas Hull, for one—a genuinely bad poet—called his collection of pathetic tales *Moral Tales in Verse* (1797) and supposed pathos to be edifying.

Unlike the pathetic tale, the preceptive tale seems to have undergone no morphological development, for it was at the end of the century what it had been at the beginning. Prior's "Hans Carvel" and Burns's "Tam o'Shanter," early and late preceptive tales, have more in common than the ninety years that separate them would seem to allow. A reading of "Tam o'Shanter" within the context of the preceptive tale is enlightening, for it is evident that "Tam o'Shanter" is innovative neither in structure, substance, nor manner; it is, on the contrary, a traditional preceptive tale. What is notable about its place in literary history is not its novelty but its fidelity to the well-established conventions of the preceptive tale. Either the preceptive tale is the tale described by Newbery or the progress tale, or it is nothing; its structure is definitive. On the other hand, the pathetic tale had a history; it underwent a number of adaptations during the course of the century.

Prior's "Henry and Emma," published in 1708 and among the earliest and certainly the most popular of pathetic tales, is a reworking of the ballad "The Not-browne Mayd," a stanzaic poem of 360 alternating tetrameter and trimeter lines; that "Henry and Emma" has nearly eight-hundred lines of heroic couplets indicates the expansion that the story underwent in Prior's hands. Like its prototype, "Henry and Emma" is a dialogue between two lovers, but Prior's poem is equipped with a two-hundred-line narrative frame, missing in the ballad, which informs the reader at length that Henry loves Emma and Emma, who has no idea at all who Henry really is, loves Henry. In each poem the lover tests his mistress and her love with a series of preposterous charges against himself and then against her. In both poems, the young women pass the test and are rewarded at the end with an offer of marriage. Fortunately, after they throw off their humble disguise, the

heroes reveal themselves as earls' sons, and all ends well—it
is always advantageous to be an earl's son in a pathetic tale.
Emma passes each test but in a style unlike the pathetic
simplicity of the nut-brown maid. When accused of lusting
rather than loving, the girl in the ballad speaks simply:

> Yf ye take hede, it is no nede
>   Such wordes to say by me;
> For oft ye prayed, and long assayed,
>   Or I you loved, pardè.

>   (ll. 253–56)[8]

Emma, moved by passions of love and grief, replies:

> Are there not Poisons, Racks, and Flames,
>   and Swords;
> That EMMA thus must die by HENRY's Words?
> Yet what could Swords, or Poison, Racks, or Flame,
> But mangle and disjoint this brittle Frame?

>   (ll. 524–28)[9]

When the young man in the ballad has concluded the test,
he says: "Myne owne dere love, I se the prove / That ye be
kynde, and true" (ll. 313–14); but Henry says:

> Hear, solemn JOVE; and, conscious VENUS, hear;
> And Thou, bright Maid, believe Me, whilst I swear;
> No Time, no Change, no future Flame shall move
> The well-plac'd Basis of my lasting Love.
> O Powerful Virtue! O Victorious Fair!

>   (ll. 633–37)

The ballad works for understatement in the language
that men do use; "Henry and Emma" works deliberately for
overstatement, for in elevating the diction, Prior believed
that he exalted both his characters and his reader, and he
was right. The effect that this poem had on the adolescent
reader in the eighteenth century was recalled by the aged
Lady Mary Wortley Montagu: "I was so much charm'd at

fourteen with the Dialogue of Henry and Emma, I can say it by heart to this Day, without refflecting [sic] on the monstrous folly of the story in plain prose. . . . This senseless Tale is, however, so well varnish'd with melody of Words and pomp of Sentiments, I am convince'd [sic] it has hurt more Girls than ever were injur'd by the lewdest Poems extant."[10] However, it failed to move Samuel Johnson, who had dismissed "Hans Carvel" as not "over decent," but who found "Henry and Emma" a "dull and tedious dialogue" and a most pernicious poem: "The example of Emma, who resolves to follow an outlawed murderer wherever fear and guilt shall drive him, deserves no imitation; and the experiment by which Henry tries the lady's constancy is such as must end either in infamy to her, or in disappointment to himself."[11] Johnson did not understand: the early pathetic tale offered no examples; it merely roused the passions and did not seek to subdue or direct them by application of judicious precepts.

What did Prior really think of his pathetic tale? He had already published a preceptive tale, "To a Young Gentleman in Love" (1702), six years before "Henry and Emma," that mocked the subject and the method of the later poem. Its subject is love; its characters are declaiming lovers — "Hope of my Age, Joy of my Youth, / Blest Miracle of Love and Truth!" (ll. 26–27).[12] But its ending is designed to undercut exalted emotions and exalted diction, for after this exchange of vows and compliments, the lover departs, and the lady "Call'd THYRSIS from beneath the Bed; / Where all this time He had been hid" (ll. 63–64). The tale concludes with a precept: "Love is a Jest; and Vows are Wind" (l. 72). There is reason, then, to doubt Prior's "sincerity" in "Henry and Emma," but it was his pathetic tale, not the preceptive one, that acquired a following in the eighteenth century.

It was at the end of a century of popularity for "Henry and Emma" that Crabbe, using the same names and the same declamatory structure, offered his rejoinder to the assumptions and style of this tale. In "The Natural Death of Love" (*Tales of the Hall*) Crabbe's Henry and Emma discover after marriage that love as they had known it in courtship is dead, inevitably so, for the charms they once saw in each other were imaginary. They have moved from a delusory world created by passion and fancy to the real world of rational choice and hard truths. The tale opens with Emma's complaints:

> *E*. Well, my good sir, I shall contend no more;
> But, O! the vows you made, the oaths you swore—
> *H*. To love you always—I confess it true;
> And do I not? If not, what can I do?[13]
>
> (ll. 109–12)

And so, like their predecessors, they declaim—rather, argue—until Henry concludes:

> What we beheld in Love's perspective glass
> Has pass'd away—one sigh! and let it pass.
> It was a blissful vision, and it fled,
> And we must get some actual good instead.
>
> (ll. 407–10)

What remains is not romantic passion but the decencies of ordinary life, friendship illuminated now and then by the transient lights of passion and fancy.

On behalf of the "real tendency of things" and the mind's operations, Crabbe repudiates the declamatory display of passion in this poem, although he adheres faithfully to the structure of the dialogue. He grants that passion raises us above our ordinary selves, but the passion ended, we must return to ordinary life, where unreal charms meet a real end. If the marriage of Crabbe's Henry and Emma is to be happy, pathos must yield to ethos, and the once infatuated pair must become good friends. Here, in this tale, where Crabbe seems to come closest to the basic terms of the pathetic narrative, his divergence from its assumptions and values is most evident, for within the form of the eighteenth century's leading pathetic tale, he states his opposition to the psychological and moral grounds on which it rests. In the interest of passion, Prior radically changed the style of the ballad, and in changing its style, he changed its structure; the ballad stanza yields to the declamatory verse paragraph, which can be as long as the passion it expresses is powerful. The aria, if you will, replaces the song. In the mid-sixties Goldsmith, Percy, and later Edmund Cartwright returned, however, to the ballad stanza but brought to it the conventions of the pathetic tale, refined by nearly half a century's diligence. In their three poems, published within a six-year period, a pattern is clearly evident. A hermit, withdrawn from the world, reveals his identity in a moment of irresistible passion to the person most concerned. In Goldsmith's "Edwin and Angelina" (1765), probably the first of these experiments, a wandering stranger, given refuge by a hermit, turns out to be a girl who tells the hermit how she jilted the excellent Edwin, who betook himself to a hermit's cell and there, it is believed, perished. She seeks his grave, hoping to expire there herself. The hermit's disclosure of himself as Edwin and the ensuing reversal of fortune follow at once:

> The hermit cried,
> And clasp'd her to his breast.
> Th' astonish'd fair-one turn'd to chide,
> 'Twas EDWIN's self that prest.
>
> (ll. 141–44)[14]

An encounter, a speech, a discovery, and happiness. Passion produces declamation and declamation, truth; truth produces a discovery and discovery, a happy reversal.

This pattern is to be found in Percy's "The Friar of Orders Grey" (1765). In Cartwright's "Armine and Elvira" (1771)—longer, busier, more populous than Goldsmith's and Percy's tales—another hermit (an earl, of course) has withdrawn from the great world, taking with him his only son, the seeming-rustic Armine. The hermit declaims his own story at length to Armine and, as a late-eighteenth-century hermit should, moralizes fluently. And Armine? As Henry loved Emma, and Emma loved Henry, so do Armine and Elvira love one another. Mingling declamations one day, the young lovers are surprised by her haughty father: "My daughter! heavens! it cannot be— / And yet it must—O dire disgrace! / . . . Clasp'd in a peasant's vile embrace!" (Pt.II, ll. 287–90).[15] The sudden appearance of the irate Father-Earl-Hermit produces a by-now-familiar turn and discovery:

> "His peasant soul!"—indignant fire
>   Flash'd from the conscious father's eye,
> "A gallant earl is Armine's sire,
>   "And know, proud chief, that earl am I.
>
> "Tho' here, within the hermit's cell,
>   "I long have liv'd unknown to fame,
> "Yet crouded camps and courts can tell—
>   "Thou too hast heard of Egbert's name."
>
> "Hah! Egbert! he, whom tyrant rage
>   "Forc'd from his country's bleeding breast?
> "The patron of my orphan age,
>   "My friend, my warrior stands confest!"
>   (Pt. II, ll. 318–26)

All problems solved, the passions of joy, gratitude, and wonder attend the marriage of Armine and Elvira.

In these poems, which are among the leading literary ballads of the eighteenth century, the poets did not propose to create an antiquarian ballad on the order of Thomas Chatterton's; rather, each wished to exploit the properties of the ballad for pathetic effects. The poets employed the ballad stanza but substituted the structure of the pathetic tale for that of the ballad. All worked with hermits, too, but how unlike Parnell's hermit these are! His goes out into the world to question, participate, and act; these withdraw into solitude, their story awaiting the first access of passion to be told. When the right character appears, the necessary discovery is made, and the tale is told and ended.

Like "Henry and Emma" and like "Edwin and Angelina," James Thomson's "Palemon and Lavinia" (1730) in *Autumn* neither offered nor pretended to offer a useful lesson but celebrated in highly ornamental language the passions of virtuous folk. Newbery considered it both "pathetick" and "pleasing,"[16] but the editor included it in *Beauties of English Poetry* under protest: "it is rather given here for being much esteemed by the public than the editor."[17] Under the burden of the florid style, the plot of "Palemon and Lavinia," tenuous in any circumstance, disappears, carrying with it, out of sight and out of mind, anything that might be called delineation of character. This tale is a gathering of beauties around a single incident, which is focused on a discovery and reversal of fortune; it is held together by poetic justice and an elevation of tone that is achieved by heavy ornament and impassioned declamation.

The rustic Lavinia, young but poor, one day goes to glean Palemon's fields. Palemon sees her, supposes her a peasant, falls in love at once, wishes she were the late Acasto's daughter—she is Acasto's daughter and she promptly, though blushingly, accepts her employer's sudden offer of marriage. That is the action of the tale; Lavinia's poverty has stretched far into the past, and her happiness stretches indefinitely into the future. The action itself is limited to a few minutes, during which the necessary, if improbable, passions come into play; the right words are uttered, and the inevitable discovery and happy reversal ensue—the machinery of happiness. Virtue and passion have their reward.

> She looks, methinks,
> Of old Acasto's line; and to my mind

Recalls that patron of my happy life,
From whom my liberal fortune took its rise,—
. . . .
Romantic wish, would this the daughter were!
(ll. 241–52, *passim*)[18]

She *is*. Here Thomson is significantly perspicuous, for circumstances of action and character are suppressed while ornament and declamation govern:

When, strict inquiring, from herself he found
She was the same, the daughter of his friend,
Of bountiful Acasto. . . .

Then the ornamenting passions appear:

who can speak
The mingled passions that surprised his heart
And through his nerves in shivering transport ran?
. . . .
Love, gratitude, and pity wept at once.
(ll. 255–60, *passim*)

And as soon as they appear, declamation begins. Palemon pours out "the pious rapture of his soul": "Acasto's dear remains? . . . O . . . Sweeter than Spring! . . . surviving blossom . . . ! . . . say, ah where . . . ? wind . . . rain . . . keen . . . tender years . . . Oh, let me . . . pride and joy!" (ll. 265–81, *passim*). The story moves swiftly to its happy ending:

Nor waited he reply. Won by the charm
Of goodness irresistible, and all
In sweet disorder lost, she blushed consent.
(ll. 298–300)

What is significant about Lavinia is that, since she set out that day "with smiling patience in her looks," she has done nothing but blush. Palpably, she is a modest girl, but, more important, she is a notably mindless one. Lavinia neither reasons nor chooses, for the mind, with its faculties for ethical choice, has disappeared in favor of simple and simplifying passions that were designed, in their display, to rouse the eighteenth-century reader's own. Parnell's tale is directed simultaneously toward the reader's eye and mind, but Thomson's is directed toward the heart. In Parnell's tale, the passions visibly agitate the mind of the hermit; in Thomson's, they replace the mind of the character and the reader.

Parnell had demonstrated that the verse tale requires both tact and judgment if it is to be effectively managed. He was successful because he carefully adjusted the circumstances to the responses he wished to represent or to elicit; he brought action, object, mind, and feeling to the reader's eye but did not overburden his narratives with particulars or with ornament. In Thomson's tale the passions and their appropriate ornaments are larger than anything so slight a form as the verse tale can support. Given the choice in the narrow boundaries of the verse tale between elevation and perplexity, declamation and action, ornament and description, Thomson invariably chooses the first. In "Palemon and Lavinia" the task of carrying forward the plot—if this tale may be said to have one—is assigned, not surprisingly, to declamations of the enraptured Palemon; Lavinia has not a word to say for herself. Producing neither perplexity nor suspense in the reader, the pathetic tale's direction is always upward: impassioned exaltation of characters and readers. Thus incident is reduced and simplified. Given these terms, Thomson wisely suppresses the details of physical action. The later example of Anna Seward's *Louisa* will indicate what happens when passionate action is brought to the eye in impassioned language.

The structure of the pathetic tale admits almost indefinite expansion. More and longer ornaments and declamations can produce almost voluminous tales. Then, too, in some of the later pathetic tales the off-stage fable is more complicated than it is in Prior's or Thomson's tales. This was easily done: the poet did not have to represent the story in incidents; he needed only to have his characters talk about it. The plot lies in the past, impinging on but still outside the structure of the declaiming present: characters now simply have more to talk about than in earlier pathetic tales. David Mallet's "Amyntor and Theodora: or, the Hermit" offers an example. Transformed from a drama into a lengthy pathetic tale, "Amyntor and Theodora" accommodated itself readily to its new genre, nor is that surprising, for in the pathetic tale the poet was trying to achieve in declamation the immediate pathos of tragedy without, of course, the unhappy ending. Mallet's poem opens in the Hebrides, where a hermit witnesses a shipwreck with only one apparent survivor, a young man whose intended bride *seems* to have perished in the wreck. Of course, the bride-to-be is the hermit's daughter and the young man is the son of the man who drove the hermit to his hermitage—and of course, the girl turns out not to be dead. These discoveries are made in the usual excited manner, although Mallet adds the sublime Thomsonian landscape to his tale; description at times may obscure, but it does not stop the flow of impassioned speech. Lengthy descriptions and a more complicated fable amplify the pathetic tale without changing its structure.

Around 1770, however, a change occurs; before that time the poet had two alternatives: a simple exchange of declamations by two or more speakers within a relatively subordinate narrative frame (as in "Henry and Emma") or a more fully developed narrative frame presented by a speaker not directly involved in the events he relates (as in "Palemon and Lavinia"). In William Richardson's "Rowena" (1774) and in Anna Seward's *Louisa: A Poetical Novel* (1784) as well as in two of Crabbe's early published tales, "Sir Eustace Grey" and "The Hall of Justice" (*Poems,* 1807), the narrating voice of the tale is that of its leading character. The tale itself becomes a declamation, in the manner of Pope's "Eloisa."

Brief and yet elevated, passionate, declaiming, and reminiscent in its style and organization, "Rowena" begins with a question:

> Why, lovely daughter of the vale, descend
> Thy tears fast-trickling? To the desart-gale
> Flow thy disheveled tresses? On thy cheek
> Fades the young rose with pining grief. Dispel
> Thy rising fears, nor wildly-gazing turn
> Incessant to the vacant shapeless air
> Thine eye disordered.
>
> (p. 123)[19]

Rowena weeps and gazes wildly because she sees a ghost of a dead lover, and her answer to the question is the tale. Edwin ("gentle . . . / But if enraged, wild") loves Rowena, but Edred ("skilled in guileful arts, he . . . / Whispered studied tales / To the believing virgins") flirts with Rowena. There is a duel, leaving both Edwin and Edred cursing Rowena as they die. (pp. 124–25). The pathos hitherto reserved for the declamations of the characters now colors the entire tale.

Crabbe's "Sir Eustace Grey" and "The Hall of Justice," both pathetic narratives, are similar to "Rowena" in several respects. "Sir Eustace Grey" is probably Crabbe's most elevated and declamatory tale. Like Rowena, Sir Eustace Grey, the madman, is at once the speaker and the leading character in this tale, and he, too, is exalted by a pathological excitement as he relates his story and describes his sufferings. Sir Eustace Grey, like Rowena, stops short of the usual pathetic discovery and so both speakers exist permanently in the heightened condition that is common to the characters in all pathetic tales before their impassioned words produce the discovery and reversal. There is no resolution of the problem or diminution of the intensity with which the ghost-haunted Rowena and the hallucinated Sir Eustace speak:

> It would the stoutest heart dismay,
>   To see, to feel, that dreadful sight;

So swift, so pure, so cold, so bright,
  They pierced my frame with icy wound,
And, all that half-year's polar night,
  Those dancing streamers wrapp'd me round.[20]

(ll. 222–27)

The whole of Crabbe's tale defines the complicated process that deranged Sir Eustace's mind as well as the intricate self-delusions by means of which this madman can convince himself that he is now perfectly sane. There is no hope for Rowena because Edred and Edwin, though their names may suggest it, are not hermits or earls' sons—they are dead; there is no hope for Sir Eustace because the process that has ruined his mind is irreversible. Sir Eustace will not recover his sanity, but it is a symptom of his madness that he now believes that he has recovered it. The mind works in accord with the real tendency of things, and the real tendency of things carries Sir Eustace Grey beyond hope.

In the other tale by Crabbe in *Poems*, "The Hall of Justice," a lifetime, like a mind, must submit to "things as they are." This tale begins:

VAGRANT

Take, take away thy barbarous hand,
  And let me to thy master speak;
Remit awhile the harsh command,
  And hear me, or my heart will break.

MAGISTRATE

Fond wretch! and what canst thou relate,
  But deeds of sorrow, shame, and sin?
Thy crime is proved, thou know'st thy fate;
  But come, thy tale!—begin, begin!—[21]

(Pt. I, ll. 1–8)

The old woman, holding a child in her arms, proceeds to give her impassioned account of her history. Raped in her youth by her lover's father, she conceived a child, a girl, who was later abandoned—the mother of the child she now holds. After years of prostitution and vagrancy, she met her daughter in a prison:

> She knew my name—we met in pain;
>   Our parting pangs can I express?
> She sail'd a convict o'er the main,
>   And left an heir to her distress.
> This is that heir to shame and pain,
>   For whom I only could descry
> A world of trouble and disdain—
>   Yet, could I bear to see her die . . . ?
>
> (Pt. II, ll. 97–104)

Using the declamatory method, Crabbe shifts the terms of the pathetic tale. Ordinarily the encounter between mother and daughter—the happy discovery and reversal—would have been the end toward which the whole narrative moved, but in this tale it is only one event in a series that constitutes this woman's hard lot. The real tendencies of things assert themselves and go relentlessly on, changing the structure of the tale as they proceed. Crabbe uses the pathetic declamation to lacerate the reader, not to please him: there are the pains of sympathy, as there are its pleasures. "The Hall of Justice" is not the kind of pathetic tale that Crabbe's contemporaries expected; the old woman's story is so intrinsically painful that the reader can hardly enjoy the self-approbation that virtuous sympathy ought to afford. Crabbe appropriates a popular genre, but his attitude toward his material makes for a radical change in the genre itself—in this instance, an event long overdue in the history of the pathetic tale.

In Anna Seward's *Louisa* the enamored and long-suffering but ultimately happy Eugenio and Louisa tell their story at some length in four declamatory epistles. Seward called her poem a "poetical novel" and identified its prototypes as "Henry and Emma" and Pope's "Eloisa." *Louisa* was intended to be a "description of passions rather than incidents."[22] The language of *Louisa* is appropriately elevated and "rich"—beyond belief so. There is little point in reciting the events of this trifling yet ponderous narrative; suffice it to say, woe is articulate and the ending happy. Incidents, as Anna Seward believed they ought to be, are relegated to the backstairs; the present is the time for passion, not action:

> An ingenious Friend, after reading the first epistle, remarked that LOUISA might have described with more interesting particularity her Lover's declaration of his passion, and the manner in which she received that declaration; but the Author thought the present method of conveying that circumstance to the mind of the Reader more poetic. POPE's ELOISA is minute in her description of the awful Scenery . . . , but by no means minute concerning the amorous eclaircissement between herself and Abelard. [p. i]

The incidents Seward does bring to the eye are those of the intenser kind—a woman scorning husband and child, a deathbed, and a near-rape, subjects appropriate to that style to which its author had become accustomed:

> Alarm'd, the Villains quit their struggling
>   Prey,
> And two, with terror struck, speed fast away.
> Fiercer the third, the arm of blood extends;
> The levell'd tube, in dire direction, bends!
> Yet no cold fear arrests my vengeful force,
> And his wing'd death-ball flies with erring course;
> But not descends my nervous blow in vain,
> The hidden lead indents the Murd'rer's brain;
> With one demoniac glance, as down he fell,
> The Soul starts furious from its vital cell.

> (p. 32)

True, Seward was writing a poetical novel and thus was heir to large, if confused, privileges. Even so, one recalls Parnell's narrative brevity with something like wonder:

> . . . the younger crept,
> Near the clos'd cradle where an infant slept,

And writh'd his neck: the landlord's little pride,
O strange return! grew black, and gasp'd, and dy'd.[23]

As the century wears on, the quotations noticeably grow longer. As Anna Seward said: "Brevity is by *no means* the chief excellence of poetry. . . . Ah! surely no brief condensing into one general image—no single comparison, however bold and exalted, could so deeply impress the mind as these felicities of poetic amplification."[24]

I think that Anna Seward would have regarded Crabbe's verse tales as "grovelling"—hers was a higher flight. In "The Mother" (*Tales in Verse*) Crabbe deals with a situation similar to that of *Louisa*. However, for Crabbe, the marriage of a faithless lover to another woman is no proof of inordinate sensibility or act of virtuous self-sacrifice; it is, instead, the consequence of weakness and vanity, of a day-by-day process in which frustrated love gives way first to petulance and then to self-interest. "The Mother" ends with the young man unhappily married, the girl he wanted to marry dead, and the girl's mother, the person who prevented the marriage, unchanged, as selfish, proud, and complacent as ever. There is a deathbed scene in "The Mother," but it serves no one's convenience, leads to no amorous éclaircissement. Nonetheless, though Anna Seward and Crabbe regarded and treated their subjects differently, they shared them. For example, Louisa learns of Eugenio's marriage from the pages of a newspaper:

Now glooms on the stain'd page the barb'rous
        Truth,
And blights each blooming promise of my youth!
EUGENIO *married*!—Anguish, and Despair,
In ev'ry pompous killing letter glare!
Thy Love, a Sacrifice to glut thy Pride!—
Ah! what avail the riches of thy Bride!

(p. 17)

In Crabbe's tale, the mother triumphantly shows the forsa-

ken girl the commonplace newspaper article announcing
the young man's marriage:

> The mother cried—"Behold your constant boy—
> "Thursday—was married—take the paper, sweet,
> "And read the conduct of your reverend cheat;
> "See with what pomp of coaches, in what crowd
> "The creature married—of his falsehood proud!
> "False, did I say?—at least no whining fool;
> . . . .
> "But shall his bride your single state reproach?
> "No! give him crowd for crowd, and coach for coach."[25]
>
> (ll. 244–52)

However, no matter how similar the subjects, the mental
processes that Crabbe represented could not be adapted to
the structure of the pathetic tale, nor could the states of
mind he delineated be other than falsified by the elevated
diction of this genre.

The pathetic tale carried over into the first decade of the
nineteenth century. Robert Bloomfield, for one, wrote
pathetic tales and published them in *Rural Tales* (1802).
Although Bloomfield hoped that there was "moral merit" in
these tales, morality is difficult to extract from these insipid
compositions about humble passions and homely virtues.[26]
His intentions are many degrees below those of Seward or
Mallet, and he attempts something of a return to the mean
diction that his subject authorized. Nonetheless, passion is
there to fire the speakers and ornament enriches the tale.
Declamation heightens it and declamation resolves it, but in
a tone and in terms that are alien to those of the earlier
pathetic tale, although rather like those which one sometimes encounters in Crabbe's worst moments:

> "I know your history, and your wishes know;
> "And love to see the seeds of Virtue grow.
> "I've a spare Shed that fronts the public road:

"Make that your Shop; I'll make it your abode.
"Thus much from me,—the rest is but your due."

(p. 28)

As in the earlier pathetic tales, the solution to seeming
difficulties stands waiting in the wings to be declaimed, to be
brought into the impassioned and troubled present. Walter
and Jane, like Edwin and Angelina, Palemon and Lavinia,
Eugenio and Louisa, and Armine and Elvira, will marry,
even though the terms of their story are so "low" that declamation loses its elevation in this unsuccessful attempt to
render the simple pathos of humble lives.

Bloomfield descended to the agricultural laboring classes
for his pathetic heroes; Sir Walter Scott moved back into the
past for his tales, and it was more Scott's intention to describe that past than to declaim about it. *Marmion* may be
characterized as a series of episodes arising naturally out of
the scenery. It nonetheless belongs to the genre of the
pathetic tale, for whatever unity its far-flung and scarcely
integrated episodes may have is derived from the events
that occurred before the beginning of the tale. Whatever we
learn about this eventful past, we learn from declamations
scattered from one end of Scotland to another, each telling
us about events whose consequences are supposedly still
operating in the present—but they fail to operate, and the
tragic-happy ending is reached when all the persons in the
narrative travel off in different directions on different er-
rands and happen upon the battle of Flodden Field.[27] Yet
the prevailing emphasis is on description, not on declamation: the real purpose of *Marmion* is, after all, to afford the
reader a scenic journey through sixteenth-century Scotland, the story of Marmion's misdeeds and his errand serving only to justify and vary the scenery. What is particularly
interesting in *Marmion* is Scott's reliance on eighteenth-
century descriptive techniques and his carrying these to
an extreme that not even Gay essayed, although in Gay's
strong and Gothic emphasis on scene as the controlling

value in narrative, one can see the inevitability of *Marmion*. At the same time, *Marmion* demonstrates again the adaptability of the pathetic tale—its capacity for lending itself, it seems, to almost anything, even though on this occasion, the tale is directed more toward the reader's eye than his sympathizing heart.

The popularity of *Marmion*, coming at the beginning of the nineteenth century, indicates that the pathetic tale was still active, though being put to new uses. The question now to be considered is how did Crabbe in his more characteristic and later tales exploit this genre? In "Sir Eustace Grey" and "The Hall of Justice" he attempted to work with a "pure" version of the pathetic tale and then gave up the experiment. Crabbe was aware of the alternative afforded him by the pathetic tale. Yet it was an alternative that he subordinated to other intentions when he chose to employ it—witness his Henry and Emma in "The Natural Death of Love." "Jesse and Colin" is the most "pathetic" in structure and tone of the tales in *Tales in Verse;* even so, it is closer in substance and representational method to Maria Edgeworth's prose tales than to any pathetic verse tale that I have read.

"Jesse and Colin," consisting largely of declamations, is built upon the contrast of life in the houses of the poor but generous and of the rich and selfish. Having made the wrong choice and rejected the poor but generous Colin of the title, Jesse is then exposed—by means of a series of declamations—to the characters of the rich and selfish and their hangers-on. By the time she has heard them out, she is ready for the cheerful poverty of Colin's cottage. Agitated by fear and anger, her mind nevertheless has remained incorruptible, and in her determination to keep it that way resides the action and unity of the tale. In the meantime, declamations of a very different sort have been going on between Colin and his virtuous mother. These are speeches of the true pathetic variety, and were we reviewers of 1812, we could sympathize readily with these people, for they offer virtues and passions that attract affection and esteem. The other crew—the rich and their toadies—are painfully common and disgusting; they harm only themselves and fail to elevate the reader above the ordinary meanness they exemplify. Indeed, they are too much like real life. In this respect, one sees a primary difference between Crabbe's tales and the tales of the pathetic narrators. In "Jesse and Colin" an old form is brought to bear upon a new subject, but the subject and the concerns it implies change the form itself.

Were this tale truly pathetic, the declamations would be directed toward entirely different ends. There would be no spying, scandal-mongering, and petty intrigues among the dependents of the rich woman. The declamations, moreover, would tell of events in the past that it was the business of the present to resolve in a few apostrophes and exclamations. The opening speech of the widow would refer to a long-lost sister, who, when last seen, held a babe in her arms—a male child. Succeeding declamations would reveal the identity of that boy, who would prove to be Colin. The tale would conclude with the reconciliation of the two sisters and a marriage that would combine the advantages of permanent happiness and affluence, for in pathetic tales the good things of this world go, in the end, to the virtuous and the impassioned. Crabbe avoids this alternative in this the most pathetic tale in *Tales in Verse*. He chooses, instead, to inculcate an implicit moral: minds can be corrupted, and the mind can resist corruption. Nor is that all. The declamations reflect, not the passions in and of themselves, but the degree to which the malicious will can affect the mind, and the principle that holds these declamations together is the responding, judging, choosing mind of the heroine.

When one compares "Jesse and Colin" to Maria Edgeworth's "The Contrast," a prose tale published in 1804, it is evident that Crabbe put the pathetic declamation to a use that was very close to that of the dialogue in prose fiction. For example, the rich woman in Crabbe's tale speaks:

"Have I not power to help you, foolish maid?
"To my concerns be your attention paid;
"With cheerful mind th' allotted duties take,
"And recollect I have a will to make."
. . . .
"Think you, fair madam, that you came to share
"Fortunes like mine without a thought or care?
"A guest indeed! from every trouble free,
"Dress'd by my help, with not a care for me."
. . . .
Jesse her thanks upon the morrow paid,
Prepar'd to go, determin'd, though afraid.
"Ungrateful creature," said the lady, "this
"Could I imagine?—are you frantic, miss?
"What! leave your friend, your prospects—is it
    true?"
This Jesse answered by a mild "Adieu!"
. . . .
The angry matron her attendant Jane
Summon'd in haste to soothe the fierce disdain.
"A vile detested wretch!" the lady cried,
"Yet shall she be, by many an effort, tried,
"And, clogg'd with debt and fear, against her will
    abide;
"And, once secured, she never shall depart
"Till I have proved the firmness of her heart;
"Then when she dares not, would not, cannot go,
"I'll make her feel what 'tis to use me so."[28]

(ll. 345–411, *passim*)

There is a comparable situation in Edgeworth's prose
tale, less heightened in tone, less contingent on malice, and,
of course, less concentrated and circumstantial than
Crabbe's poem. In "The Contrast" the irritable, hypochon-
driacal mistress and the virtuous serving-maid struggle for
dominance and freedom:

"What! You will leave me! Leave me contrary to my
orders! Take notice then: these doors you shall never
enter again, if you leave me now," cried Mrs.
Crumpe. . . . She started up in her bed, and growing

quite red in the face, cried, "Leave me now, and you leave me for ever. Remember that! Remember that!"

"Then, madam, I must leave you for ever," said Patty, moving toward the door. . . .

"The girl's an idiot!" cried Mrs. Crumpe. "After this you cannot expect that I should remember you in my will."

"No, indeed, madam; I expect no such thing," said Patty. (Her hand was on the lock of the door as she spoke.)

"Then," said Mrs. Crumpe, "perhaps you will think it worth your while to stay with me, when I tell you I have not forgot you in my will." . . .

"Oh, madam, consider my poor brother. I am sorry to disoblige you for ever . . . ," said Patty. The lock of the door turned quickly in her hand. . . . Mrs. Crumpe tried to compose herself again to sleep, but she could not; and in half an hour's time she rang the bell violently, took her purse out of her pocket, counted out twenty bright guineas, and desired . . . that her steward should gallop after Patty, and offer her that *whole sum in hand* if she would return. "Begin with one guinea, and bid on till you come up to her price," said Mrs. Crumpe. "Have her back again I will, if it were only to convince myself that she is to be had for money as well as other people."[29]

Crabbe and Edgeworth, both related to the satirist and their work to his purposes, represent minds in action in the circumstances of everyday life. "Mind" and "everyday life" are precisely what make the difference between Crabbe's tales and the pathetic tales. As Josephine Miles has said, there was a shift from ethos to pathos in the eighteenth century, from choice and initiative to suffering and endurance.[30] It is significant, then, that Crabbe attributes the power of choice to his characters—the faculties of reasoning and willing; he predicates minds for them. In his tales it is of the essence that the passions deceive the reason and pervert the will and that, after a gradual accumulation of these "impulses," habits are formed that master both will and reason. Nonetheless, the capacity for choice—for ethos—is there at least initially, although external circumstances or passionate impulse might be such as to insure that it will be the wrong choice. Here, as elsewhere, Crabbe aligns himself with the ethical tradition. What interested the pathetic narrative poet was the immediate, overwhelming, irresistible force that passion exerted upon character. Compelled by their passions, the characters in a pathetic tale could not choose but could only feel, and therein lay their interest. Once filled, animated, and elevated by the grand natural passions of love and hope or anger and grief, they naturally gave vent to their feelings in language necessarily exalted and impassioned, and, this, according to theory, ought, in turn, to rouse the reader's own passions.

Still, there is a point at which Crabbe and the writers of the pathetic tale do meet. He did not reject the assumption that the passions in their moments of greatest intensity were powerful, even overwhelming, forces, nor would he have denied that it was their tendency to elevate. He did, however, refuse to make these assumptions the basis of his narrative art, although in the principal incidents of many of his tales, his characters act under the impulse of powerful but never simple passion. There, conventionally enough, he resorts to declamation and to the representation of impassioned gestures as he seeks to convey the force of passions driving his characters and to move his reader by this representation. Yet even at his most intense, Crabbe never essays a style as heightened as that of the pathetic tale; he does raise the level of his style at such moments to a degree that is often discordant with the tone of the whole tale. He was, I think, uneasy when working with the declamation, but felt himself forced to use it, though he never mastered it. It should be remembered, too, that Crabbe's principal incidents, declamatory as they may be, are the moral as well as emotional consequence of a long and subtle process that may be characterized in traditional terms as the voluntary corruption of reason by passion. The climax toward which

he directs his narrative is pathos, but he arrives there b
means of ethos.

As the mind, with its complement of powers, invariabl
distinguishes Crabbe's tales from the genre of the patheti
tale, so it is its adaptability that distinguishes the patheti
from the preceptive tale. "There are," George Kubler ha
said, "few events in the history of the button; there are onl
variants in shape, size, and decoration; there is no duratio
in respect to difficulties encountered and overcome."[31] I
more than one way, the history of the eighteenth-centur
preceptive tale resembles that of the button. Inherent in th
species is an invariable purpose that inhibits transforma
tion: the preceptive tale may be serious or comic, bawdy o
chaste, or it may represent events fully in incident o
rapidly in summary, but its action must arise from or giv
rise to a precept. Then its practitioners never forgot that i
was a minor poem. There was, in short, a presuppositio
about the relation of narrative substance and structure t
ethical purpose that predetermined the preceptive tale'
representational alternatives. The affective purpose of th
pathetic narrative was widely recognized in the eighteent
century; yet the pathetic tale was regarded as much more o
an open question than was the preceptive tale, nor did it
practitioners always care to proceed as if it were a mino
genre. Too often claiming something high, the pathetic tale
ended by being silly—silly, but collectively significant. The
history of the pathetic tale—for it has one—is a movement
toward synthesis, toward the merging of what had once
been separate and consciously kept so: moralizing and
emotionalizing, describing and declaiming. Moreover, in
this kind of narrative important shifts and displacements
occur during the course of the century; amplification is
preferred to perspicuity, the comic low is replaced by a new
tragic low, with the humble private life demanding an elevation of tone that had once been the occasion for burlesque.
The history of the pathetic tale is the disintegration of a
whole consciousness of what is appropriate. Let loose upon

narrative verse, the pathetic poet dissolved, blurred, confused the remains of a failing tradition of Aristotelian and Horatian values with the declamatory and descriptive emphases of Longinian art.

5

PROSE FICTION

In order to understand Crabbe's narrative art, it is necessary to examine the relation that his work bears to the prose fiction of his time. A number of critics and scholars—chiefly Jeffrey, Sigworth, Speirs, and Kroeber—have observed, though only in passing, that this relationship exists: "many of the stories," Jeffrey says, "may be ranked by the side of the inimitable tales of Miss Edgeworth; and are calculated to do nearly as much good among that part of the population with which they are principally occupied."[1] Crabbe was a voracious reader of novels, a not entirely disinterested one; his son recalled that "even from the most trite of these fictions, he could sometimes catch a train of ideas that was turned to excellent use; so that he seldom passed a day without reading part of some such work, and was never very select in the choice of them."[2] More than that, around the turn of the century he wrote three novels, which he then proceeded to destroy. His son remembered that the first novel he wrote

> was entitled "The Widow Grey"; but I recollect nothing of it except that the principal character was a benevolent

humourist. . . . The next was called "Reginald Glanshaw, or the Man who commanded Success"; a portrait of an assuming, overbearing, ambitious mind, rendered interesting by some generous virtues, and gradually wearing down into idiotism. I cannot help thinking that this Glanshaw was drawn with very extraordinary power; but the story was not well-managed in the details. I forget the title of his third novel; but I clearly remember that it opened with a description of a wretched room, similar to some that are presented in his poetry. (Crabbe, Jr., *Life*, p. 47)

Anyone who is familiar with Crabbe's poetry will see at once that the poet Crabbe and the novelist Crabbe worked with the same material: in either capacity he traced the turns and movements of the heart and mind. The unpublished novels were, I believe, experiments undertaken by Crabbe in his search for a form that would carry what he knew and wished to say, one congenial to his training and principles and still significant to his contemporaries. The narrative poet assimilated the experience of the unpublished novelist. That is not all, however. The clearly discernible ties between verse satire and the kind of novels that Crabbe's contemporaries were writing during the 1790s requires consideration. Precisely because of his loyalty to the values inherent in satire, Crabbe found the late-century novel certainly an attractive, indeed a logical solution to his problems.

Although satiric poetry had failed as a "serious" poetic genre during the course of the second half of the eighteenth century, the subjects and purposes of the satirist had not been abandoned. The novelist who represented the minds and manners of his time assumed in part the satirist's role. It was generally held during the eighteenth century that representations of "existing character" and contemporary life were the proper province of verse satire; the writers of one school of prose fiction and Crabbe adopted these grounds as their own. As the "manners and characters which occur in ordinary life" were the subjects of satire, so for the novel

> Imitations of life and character have been made their principal object. Relations have been professed to be given of the behaviour of persons in particular[ly] interesting situations, such as may actually occur in life; by means of which, what is laudable or defective in character and conduct, may be pointed out, and placed in an useful light.[3]

The novelists themselves, from Defoe and Richardson on, repeat in one preface after another that "this work is addressed to the public as a history of *life* and *manners*. . . ."[4] Elizabeth Inchbald, writing in 1807, defines the novel's useful ends, its interest in ordinary life, its affinity with earlier verse satire:

> Let her therefore read certain well-written novels, and she will receive intimation of two or three foibles, the self-same as those, which, adhering to her conduct, cast upon all her virtues a degree of ridicule. — These failings are beneath the animadversions of the pulpit. They are so trivial, yet so awkward, that neither sermons, history, travels, nor biography, could point them out with propriety. . . .
> And what book so well as a novel, could show to the enlightened Lord Henry——the arrogance of his extreme condescension? Or insinuate to the judgment of Lady Eliza——the wantonness of her excessive reserve? . . .
> That Prebendary is merciful to a proverb—excluding negligence towards holy things—of which he thinks himself the holiest. Certain novels might make these people think a second time.[5]

Inchbald advocates holding a mirror up to life—Boileau's satiric mirror—so that the reader can recognize his own foibles and vices and be instructed accordingly. This view of the novel was widely accepted during the early years of the nineteenth century, as a casual reading of the reviews will readily reveal. Though the imitation of "ordinary life and manners" was no longer the business of the poet, who had more elevated tasks on hand, it is commonplace to say that novels are

> the closest imitation of men and manners; and are admitted to examine the very web and texture of society, as it really exists, and as we meet it when we come into the world. If the style of poetry has "something more divine in it," this savours more of humanity. We are brought acquainted with an infinite variety of characters . . . for the greater part, more true to general nature than those which we meet with in actual life—and have our moral impressions far more frequently called out, and our moral judgements exercised, than in the busiest career in existence.[6]

Sir Walter Scott, discussing the novels of Jane Austen, Crabbe's most distinguished admirer, observed that a "new style of novel has arisen within the last fifteen or twenty years," one relying on "the art of copying from nature as she really exists in the common walks of life, presenting to the reader, instead of the splendid scenes of an imaginary world, a correct and striking representation of that which is daily taking place around him."[7] The equivalent of this kind of novel was Flemish painting, the "low" school to which Crabbe's work was often likened. This "new style of novel" gives "accurate and unexaggerated delineations of events and characters" and replaces "formal dissertations or shorter and more desultory moral essays"; "the praise and blame of the moralist" are now "bestowed, not in general declamation, on classes of men, but on individuals representing those classes, who are so clearly delineated and brought into action before us, that we seem to be acquainted with them, and feel an interest in their fate."[8]

Truth, lowness, and usefulness are the terms common to

verse satire and the novel that these reviewers described. What Crabbe was not supposed to do as a poet, he could do as a novelist: "During one or two of his winters in Suffolk, he gave most of his evening hours to the writing of *Novels*, and he brought not less than three such works to a conclusion."[9]

Nevertheless, Crabbe concluded that he could not write a good novel and he abandoned this experiment. The tales "Sir Eustace Grey" and "The Hall of Justice," published in *Poems*, 1807, are another experiment—this time Crabbe essayed the pathetic tale—and that, too, was set aside. In *The Borough* Crabbe returned to the verse tale, having formulated at last a kind of narrative that would assimilate, without simplifying, his complex material and his equally complex attitude toward that material. He employed the progress of the eighteenth-century preceptive tale and projected the principal incident in a modified version of the declamation characteristic of the pathetic tale; but the unity, cumulative force, and sustaining strength of the tales in *The Borough* and *Tales in Verse* and *Tales of the Hall* arise from their action, an action of the mind working in accord with the real tendencies of things. Nothing like this is to be found in the verse tale in England until Crabbe's tales, yet in novels produced by members of his own generation the same principle directs the narrative. It is definitive, distinguishing their work from that of others among their contemporaries.

The novelists that mattered to Crabbe were not the Gothic novelists, who incorporated into prose narration the descriptive doctrine of poetry and who brought the least of corporeal presences, but still corporeal, to the eye, registering the movement of a tapestry or a guttering candle but not the movements of a mind. Nor is it to Fielding or Richardson or Smollett that one must look for Crabbe's fellows. The writers important to an understanding of Crabbe's narrative art are William Godwin (*Caleb Williams*, 1793), Thomas Holcroft (*The Adventures of Hugh Trevor*,

1794–1797), Elizabeth Inchbald (*Nature and Art*, 1796), and, later, Maria Edgeworth.[10] Holcroft stated their position without qualifications of any kind: "All well written books, that discuss the actions of men, are . . . histories of the progress of the mind. . . ."[11] Holcroft, whose application of this principle is a rambling history or episodic education, offers in *Hugh Trevor* obvious parallels to the subjects of several of Crabbe's tales.[12] *Caleb Williams*, as Godwin said in his preface, is a novel about "THINGS AS THEY ARE"; "it is a study and delineation of things passing in the moral world."[13] Like Holcroft, Godwin saw the actions of men as the history of mental processes, but he saw the mind's action in highly particular terms, minute in its operations and dominant in the development of plot:

> My vein of delineation, where the thing in which my imagination revelled the most freely, was the analysis of the private and internal operations of the mind, employing my metaphysical dissecting knife in tracing and laying bare the involutions of motive, and recording the gradually accumulating impulses, which led the personages I had to describe primarily to adopt the particular way of proceeding in which they afterward embarked.[14]

In the words "gradually accumulating impulses, which led the personages . . . primarily to adopt a particular way of proceeding," one finds the key not only to Godwin's and Inchbald's fiction but also to Crabbe's tales. Crabbe, like Godwin, recognized that the mind's evolution is gradual yet, in the consequences, drastic:

> Minutely trace man's life; year after year,
> Through all his days let all his deeds appear,
> And then, though some may in that life be strange,
> Yet there appears no vast nor sudden change;
> The links that bind those various deeds are seen,
> And no mysterious void is left between.

But let those binding links be all destroy'd,
All that through years he suffer'd or enjoy'd;
Let that vast gap be made, and then behold—
This was the youth, and he is thus when old;
Then we at once the work of Time survey,
And in an instant see a life's decay.[15]

(ll. 1–14)

Interestingly, almost the same terms that Godwin used to describe his own "vein of delineation" were employed by *The Christian Observer*'s reviewer in describing Crabbe's "vein," which, of course, he found sadistic:

Mr. Crabbe is a fine dissector: his moral knife lays open to universal gaze, with a firm and unshaken touch, and in horrible truth and fidelity, the breathing vitals, the *spirantia exta* of his victims. The mental sufferings he seems to take a delight in pourtraying are often worked up with a poignancy that would leave the very cruellest spectator, a Domitian himself, or a French mob, nothing to desire.[16]

Godwin's theory of the mind informs and determines the narrative of *Caleb Williams*, whose action arises from the ruling passion, complicated by a native disposition, intensified by external circumstances, and at last transformed by its exercise into an intolerable obsession. Falkland's noble mind is agitated and poisoned by the passion for "chivalric Honour"; this was "his ruling passion, the thought that worked his soul to madness." The ruling passion of Williams initially is "curiosity," in the end to be supplanted by "remorse." Falkland, driven in painful circumstances by his ruling passion, murders, then betrays, and finally persecutes. Williams, at first entangled by his curiosity, finally under the pressure of his sufferings—"the benevolence of my nature was in a great degree turned to gall"—listens in "an evil hour" to his "resentment and impatience" and betrays Falkland, only to submit to the possession of the most horrible of all ruling passions, remorse: "It was too late. The mistake I had committed was now gone, past all power of recall." The novel concludes with Falkland dead and Williams appalled by his own act: "I began these memoirs with the idea of vindicating my character. I have now no character that I wish to vindicate . . . "; he summarizes the process that destroyed both men:

> Falkland! thou enteredst upon thy career with the purest and most laudable intentions. But thou imbibedst the poison of chivalry with thy earliest youth; and the base and low-minded envy that met thee . . . operated with this poison to hurry thee into madness. Soon, too soon, by this fatal coincidence, were the blooming hopes of thy youth blasted for ever! . . . From that moment thy benevolence was, in great part, turned into rankling jealousy and inexorable precaution. Year after year didst thou spend in this miserable project of imposture; and only at last continuedst to live, long enough to see, by my misjudging and abhorred intervention, thy closing hope disappointed, and thy death accompanied with foulest disgrace! (pp. 377–78, *passim*)

J. M. S. Tompkins has found in *Caleb Williams* "what so few contemporary novels have, unity of structure and of atmosphere." Tompkins justly argues that Godwin's novel, though a novel of suspense, is by no means a Gothic novel. Suspense has for Godwin "a cogent meaning, but it was not a Gothic meaning," for suspense is contingent on the action of Williams's mind and unity is achieved precisely because Godwin concentrates on mental processes. "Mystery," as Tompkins has observed, "is not valuable in itself, but as the stimulus of Caleb's mental growth; prison and woodland provide no scenic background, and the purpose of suspense is not to enchant the reader; it is the intellectual repercussions of these conditions that are studied; they are the agents in the psychological development of Caleb":

> There is not much dialogue, and little emphasis on the single scene; but a continuous probing commentary winds itself round incident and character, and the very

impartiality with which the inquiry is conducted . . . adds to the oppression. Godwin's "metaphysical dissecting knife" lays bare the movements of intense, lonely, self-involved and tormented minds . . . and in this respect *Caleb Williams* extended the scope of the novel.[17]

Godwin and Crabbe were painting, as Trapp had said poets, by definition, must paint, the motions of the mind and the springs and movements of the heart, the tempers, passions, natures, and manners of men. They, like Inchbald in the story of Agnes Primrose in *Nature and Art*, hold to the principle that nothing must be permitted to intervene between the operations of the passions on the mind and the outcome of the story. In other words, no coincidence will intercede to save the character from the consequences of his passions and deeds, nor will poetic justice be imposed on the plot to divert it from the probable conclusion of similar events in the "real" world: things indeed as they are and only as they are. Godwin invents improbabilities in order to support this principle; everything will work in the end to trap and destroy.

Anna Letitia Barbauld, in the introduction to *The British Novelists* (1810), seems not to have recognized that an important transformation had been effected in prose fiction. "Every incident in a well written composition is introduced for a certain purpose, and made to forward a certain plan." Who would deny this? It did not occur to her that the plan could have any end other than "vice must be punished and virtue rewarded." She therefore distinguishes firmly between the conduct of the novel and "the real course of nature": "It was very probable . . . that *Gil Blas*, if a real character, would come to be hanged; but the practised novel-reader knows well that no such event can await the hero of the tale." The reader of *Tom Jones* has "no doubt but that, in spite of his irregularities and distresses, his history will come to an agreeable termination":

And why does he foresee all this? Not from the real tendencies of things, but from what he has discovered of the
author's intentions. But what would have been the prob-
ability in real life? Why . . . *Jones* would pass from one
vicious indulgence to another, till his natural good disposition was quite smothered under his irregularities—that
Sophia would either have married her lover clandestinely,
and have been poor and unhappy, or she would have
conquered her passion and married some country gentleman with whom she would have lived in moderate
happiness, according to the usual routine of married life.
But the author would have done very ill so to have con-
structed his story. If *Booth* had been a real character, it is
probable that his *Amelia* and her family would not only
have been brought to poverty, but left in it; but to the
reader it is much more probable that by some means or
other they will be rescued from it, and left in possession
of all the comforts of life.[18]

Godwin's assumptions are quite different; accordingly, he is
ready to use fiction as a means of asking and answering,
"But of what use are talents and sentiments in the corrupt
wilderness of human society? It is a rank and rotten soil,
from which every finer shrub draws poison as it grows"
(*Caleb Williams*, p. 377). Godwin, Crabbe, and Inchbald wish
to demonstrate that the system of worldly rewards is by no
means commensurate with any system of private virtue; by
no means at all will "some means or another" interfere with
the "real tendencies of things": the smothering of a good
disposition by vicious deeds or the smothering of a social
passion by a selfish one. The heroine's virtue will not be
saved; the loyal lover will not be rewarded with the lady or
her wealth; innocence will become guilty and then more
guilty; a villain will destroy innocence and then escape all
punishment but that which his own mind inflicts. That is the
"real course of nature" and that is "how things are" in the
narratives of these writers. The process is irreversible, and
if remorse comes, it comes too late. In the Gothic novel,

remorse is the given; in these novels and in many of Crabbe's tales, it is the sterile consequence toward which the work tends. The good may be shown in their goodness and the wicked blamed in their wickedness, but they are not rewarded or punished according to their desserts.

Narratives based on the system of poetic justice, in which all the difficulties are symmetrically resolved at the end, had as a means of holding the reader's interest precisely the power of fulfilling the reader's expectations step-by-step by leading him toward a conclusion that he had foreseen from the beginning. Godwin, Crabbe, and Inchbald work against that system; they violate the expectations of the reader by carrying him toward a conclusion that he might acknowledge as true to life, but, for him, not true to the established procedures of fiction. The final power that these novels and tales have is that they push matters in the direction of an entirely different kind of inevitability. One reason that critics found Crabbe's tales so "lacerating," "painful," and "disgusting" is simply that they were being dragged, against their will and against their preconceptions, over rough and unfamiliar ground, and "numbers" only intensified the difficulty.

Crabbe explicitly repudiates the system of poetic justice on more than one occasion and implicitly rejects it in all of his practice. In "Ellen Orford" (*The Borough*) the narrator complains "That books, which promise much of life to give, / Should show so little how we truly live" (ll. 15–16).[19]

> Life, if they'd search, would show them many a change,
> The ruin sudden and the misery strange!
>
> (ll. 21–22)

The generality of writers, however, seek "a single spot in fairy-ground; / Where . . . / plots are laid and histories are told" (ll. 26–28):

> These let us leave, and at her sorrows look,
> Too often seen, but seldom in a book;

Let her who felt, relate them.—On her chair
The heroine sits—in former years the fair,
Now aged and poor; but Ellen Orford knows
That we should humbly take what Heav'n bestows.

(ll. 120–25)

Then follows a tale of "real life": seduction, suicide, religious despair, idiocy, executions, incest, blindness. Crabbe represents Ellen Orford's life as it probably would happen—perhaps as it did happen—following her from youth and hope to old age and resignation. Again, in "Resentment," in *Tales in Verse*, Crabbe attacks the conventions of contemporary fiction and describes his own practice:

In vain an author would a name suppress,
From the least hint a reader learns to guess;
· ·
Our favourites fight, are wounded, hopeless lie;
Survive they cannot—nay, they cannot die:
Now, as these tricks and stratagems are known,
'Tis best, at once, the simple truth to own.
    This was the husband—in an humble shed
He nightly slept, and daily sought his bread.
Once for relief the weary man applied;
"Your wife is rich," the angry vestry cried;
Alas! he dared not to his wife complain,
Feeling her wrongs, and fearing her disdain.[20]

(ll. 305–22, *passim*)

Again, in "The Mother" (*Tales in Verse*), true love, virtue, money, all promise domestic happiness, but the selfish vanity of a girl's mother intervenes and ruins what would have been a standard ending in fiction not in accord with the real course of nature: "Yes! reason sanctions what stern fate denies . . . " (l. 172).[21] The tale ends with the prospective bridegroom married to someone else, the heroine dead, and the mother unmoved by the destruction she has caused. Remorse does not overtake this shallow nature:

"The mother lives, and has enough to buy / Th'attentive ear and the submissive eye / Of abject natures . . . " (ll. 341–43).

Godwin said, "Change the society." Crabbe said, "Accept what Heaven bestows; be resigned." But both agreed that Things as They Are is the proper subject of fiction and that Things as They Are is very hard on people with minds.

Elizabeth Inchbald agreed, too, notably in her second and last novel, *Nature and Art*, her "deeply pathetic story," which Crabbe read to his family and which they found heartbreaking because of its "associations" with persons in their neighborhood.[22]

Nature and Art attacks English society—the church, the rich, the aristocracy, the judiciary—all the respectables. The main story resembles an apologue, whereas the secondary plot is the pathetic story of Agnes Primrose that moved Crabbe's family; the work as a whole concludes with a precept, to which the subplot contributes its forceful share: "Let the poor then . . . no more be their own persecutors—no longer pay homage to wealth—instantaneously the whole idolatrous worship will cease—the idol will be broken."[23] Resembling a short tale, the subplot is easily detached from the preceptive main plot. Inchbald avoids sentimentality as she traces her heroine's destiny— she is sparing of effects, dedicated as she is to the concise and incisive. Nor does she wish to bring the whole sad story fully to the eye of the reader or to make him the spectator of anything but a few climactic incidents. Then the few, spare strokes come home, as she meant them to do. Above all, she intends to delineate the operations of Agnes Primrose's mind, to trace the gradually accumulating impulses that bring the girl to ruin. Once that is accomplished, descriptive circumstances may rouse the reader's sympathy.

Agnes Primrose, beginning as a virtuous and hopeful young woman, ends on the gallows, a prostitute and criminal. Her story is an ethical progress toward the culminating pathos of a principal incident. Seduced and abandoned by an ambitious young man, she leaves her home to support herself and her child in London. At last she is hired as a maid of all work in a brothel, and in time she becomes one of the prostitutes herself, then a streetwalker, and finally a criminal. A period of eighteen years is covered by the action, years in which passions work upon a certain temper of mind in particular circumstances. What happens may be broken into two phases. In the first of these, passions and rationalizations work upon her "pliant" mind and against her "heart" to condition her to becoming a prostitute:

> At first she shuddered at those practices she saw, at those conversations she had heard; and blest herself that poverty, not inclination, had caused her to be a witness of such profligacy, and had condemned her in this vile abode to be a servant, rather than in the lower rank of mistress. — Use softened those horrors every day — at length, self-defense, the fear of ridicule, and the hope of favour, induced her to adopt that very conduct from which her heart revolted.
>
> In her sorrowful countenance, and fading charms, there yet remained attraction for many visitors — and she now submitted to the mercenary profanations of love; more odious, as her mind had been subdued by its most captivating, most endearing joys. (p. 338)

Rationalization binds her to the choice to which habit, passion, and circumstance have brought her:

> While incessant regret whispered to her "that she ought to have endured every calamity rather than this," she thus questioned her nice sense of wrong — "Why, why respect myself, since no other respects me? Why set a value on my own feelings, when no one else does?"
>
> Degraded in her own judgment, she doubted her own understanding when it sometimes told her she had deserved better treatment — for she felt herself a fool in comparison with her learned seducer, and the rest who despised her. "And why," she continued, "should I un-

gratefully persist to contemn women, who alone are so kind as to accept me for a companion? (p. 338)

Her desire for sympathy and the good nature that this desire implies influence her conclusions and contribute to her disaster; but specious reasoning will not save her from the consequences of her acts, nor will the narrator save her:

> In speculation, these arguments appeared reasonable, and she pursued their dictates—but in the practice of the life in which she was plunged, she proved the fallacy of the system; and at times tore her hair with frantic sorrow. . . .
> But she had gone too far to recede. . . . Now, alas! the time for flying was past—all prudent choice was over—even all reflection was gone for ever—or only admitted on compulsion, when it imperiously forced its way amidst the scenes of tumultuous mirth, of licentious passion, of distracted   riot,   shameless   effrontery,   and   wild intoxication—when it *would* force its way—even through the walls of a brothel. (pp. 338–39)

Agnes Primrose's progress toward the gallows is represented as an internal action. Time passes, and other chapters concerned with the main plot intervene; then Inchbald returns to Agnes Primrose. The undescribed years have carried her from the relative dignity of the brothel to the midnight streets. The second phase of her progress begins, for she has been carried as far down in the world as prostitution can bring her. Now she must move toward death, and Inchbald makes it clear that the nature of Agnes Primrose's destiny is contingent on the nature of her mind:

> Had these miseries, common to the unhappy prostitute, been alone the punishment of Agnes—had her crimes and sufferings ended in distress like this, her story had not perhaps been selected for a public recital; for it had been no other than the customary history of thousands of her sex. But Agnes had a destiny yet more

fatal.—Unhappily, she was endowed with a mind so sen-
sibly alive to every joy, and every sorrow, to every mark of
kindness, every token of severity, so liable to excess in
passion, that, once perverted, there was no degree of
error from which it would revolt. (p. 346)

Passions and arguments, more "criminal" in their assumptions and conclusions after the hard usage of the years,
again work upon her, on this occasion to join a gang of
thieves and sharpers. In three paragraphs, Inchbald delineates the process of ratiocination, the circumstances to
which Agnes Primrose had been brought after years of suffering, and the fatal strength of her native disposition toward goodness.

> Taught by the conversation of the dissolute poor . . . or
> by her own observation on the worldly reward of elevated
> villany, she began to suspect "that dishonesty was only
> held a sin, to secure the property of the rich; and that, to
> take from those who did not want, by the art of stealing,
> was less guilt, than to take from those who did want, by
> the power of the law."
> By false, yet seducing opinions such as these, her rea-
> son estranged from every moral and religious tie, her
> necessities urgent, she reluctantly accepted the proposal
> to mix with a band of sharpers and robbers; and became
> an accomplice in negotiating bills forged on a country
> banker.
> But though ingenious in arguments to excuse the deed
> before its commission; in the act, she had ever the dread
> of some incontrovertible statement on the other side of
> the question. Intimidated by this apprehension, she was
> the veriest bungler in her vile profession—and on the
> alarm of being detected, while every one of her confed-
> erates escaped and absconded, she alone was seized—
> was arrested . . . and committed to the provincial jail . . .
> to take her trial—for life or death. (pp. 346–47)

As one might guess, her judge is the man who had seduced her. Recognition and a pardon are in order, but neither occurs. He does not know who she is, he condemns her, and she is executed. Only when it is too late does he learn her identity. Like Caleb Williams and Crabbe's villains and weaklings, he has only useless remorse ahead of him. The trial, presented in a four-and-a-half-page chapter, constitutes the principal incident of the tale of Agnes Primrose. What Inchbald has provided thus far is a progress, a summary of internal events, all accumulating and gathering force for the pathetic encounter in the courtroom. The principal incident is organized in terms of contrast, and descriptive strokes bring this contrast to the eye and heart of the reader.

> When, in the morning, she was brought to the bar, and her guilty hand held up before the righteous judgment-seat of William — imagination could not form two figures, or two situations more incompatible with the existence of former familiarity, than the judge and the culprit — and yet, these very persons had passed together the most blissful moments that either ever tasted! — Those hours of tender dalliance were now present to *her* mind — *His* thoughts were more nobly employed in his high office — nor could the haggard face, hollow eye, desponding countenance, and meager person of the poor prisoner, once call to his memory . . . his former youthful, lovely Agnes!
> She heard herself arraigned, with trembling limbs and downcast looks . . . before she ventured to lift her eyes up to her awful judge. — She then gave one fearful glance, and discovered William, unpitying but beloved William, in every feature! (pp. 348–49)

The contrast is carried back into the past, with the author stepping in to make matters clear:

> "What defense have you to make?"
> It was William spoke to Agnes! — The sound was sweet — the voice was mild, was soft, compassionate,

encouraging! ... —not such a voice as when William last addressed her; when he left her undone and pregnant. ...

She could have hung upon the present words for ever! She did not call to mind that this gentleness was the effect of practice, the art of his occupation ... —In the present judge, tenderness was not designed for the consolation of the culprit, but for the approbation of the auditors.

There were no spectators, Agnes, by your side when last he parted from you—if there had, the awful William had been awed to marks of pity. (p. 349)

As the incident continues, the particulars are sketched in with an increasing degree of specificity:

Again he put the question, and with these additional sentences, tenderly and emphatically delivered— "Recollect yourself—Have you no witnesses? No proof in your behalf?"

A dead silence followed these questions.

He then mildly, but forcibly, added—"What have you to say?"

Here, a flood of tears burst from her eyes, which she fixed earnestly upon him, as if pleading for mercy, while she faintly articulated,

"Nothing, my lord." ...

He summed up the evidence—and every time he was compelled to press hard upon the proofs against her, she shrunk, and seemed to stagger with the deadly blow— writhed under the weight of *his* minute justice, more than from the prospect of a shameful death.

The jury consulted but a few minutes—the verdict was—

"Guilty."

She heard it with composure.

But when William placed the fatal velvet on his head, and rose to pronounce her sentence—she started with a kind of convulsive motion—retreated a step or two back,

and lifting up her hands, with a scream exlaimed—
"Oh! not from *you!*" (pp. 350–51)

An exclamation which, Barbauld said, "electrifies the
reader, and cannot but stir the coldest feelings. . . . Judge-
ment and observation may sketch characters, and often put
together a good story; but strokes of pathos such as the one
just mentioned . . . can only be attained by those whom nature has endowed with her choicest gifts."[24]

The scene and chapter conclude with Agnes Primrose's
fate determined and the contrast still much in evidence:

Serene and dignified, as if no such exclamation had
been uttered, William delivered the fatal speech, ending
with—"Dead, dead, dead."
She fainted as he closed the period, and was carried
back to prison in a swoon; while he adjourned the court
to go to dinner. (p. 351)

Crabbe employs the same narrative structure in many of
his tales, particularly those in *Tales in Verse:* a series of quasi
incidents representing an internal action of the mind prog-
ressing toward and culminating in a principal incident, an
encounter of cruel contrasts; although Crabbe is working
within the limits of the couplet and the short verse tale, he
covers the same extensive and subtle ground, the working
out of a mental process that consumes a whole lifetime. Like
Inchbald, he uses contrast as the organizing principle of the
culminating incident, but, within the limits imposed by 500
or 700 lines, an even more intense kind of concentration of
material is required in Crabbe's tales. Moreover, he accepts the eighteenth century's doctrine that narrative
poetry must bring its circumstances to the eye. The question
is, how does he manage to accommodate all these intentions? First, he narrows his subject drastically, but what he
does can be understood better if we first consider one of
Maria Edgeworth's tales.

Maria Edgeworth also accepted the "real" as the decisive

term for fiction: "Did you," she asked Elizabeth Inchbald, "really draw the characters from life, or did you invent them?"; she is speaking here of Inchbald's first novel, *A Simple Story*, which she praised in these words: "I never read *any* novel—I except *none*—I never read any novel that affected me so strongly, or that so completely possessed me with the belief in the real existence of all the people it represents."[25] Scattered along the bottom margin of Edgeworth's stories are frequent footnotes stating that a certain event or detail is "real":

> It is remarkable, that several incidents which have been objected to as impossible or improbable, were true. For instance, the medical case, vol. ii. p. 217. . . .
> A bishop was really saved from suffocation by a clergyman in his diocese (no matter where or when) in the manner represented. . . . A considerable estate was about seventy years regained, as described . . . by the discovery of a sixpence under the seal of a deed.[26]

At the same time, Maria Edgeworth also upheld a system of education that, like the novels of Godwin and Inchbald and the tales of Crabbe, assumed a certain theory of the mind as its basis. However, a more important purpose intervened; this system of education must prove its efficacy: "These Tales have been written to illustrate the opinions delivered in 'Practial Eucation.' "[27] To make the system attractive, Edgeworth found poetic justice necessary. The result is that the mind and "real life" in a tale by Maria Edgeworth, excepting the early *Castle Rackrent*, must work with a narrative intention that, however efficiently and thoroughly it makes its point, is essentially at odds with its material, for at the end of a tale by Maria Edgeworth everyone is exactly where he ought to be in terms of a poetically just distribution of worldly rewards and punishments, and no one is quite where the real tendencies of things carry Agnes Primrose or Caleb Williams or the characters in Crabbe's tales. The result in Edgeworth's fiction, then, is an illustrative compound

of truth and fiction, and she often had difficulties in com-
bining the two: "Madame de Fleury is mostly true: Maria
says she has often observed that it is very difficult to make
truth and fiction mix well together."[28]

At the same time her narratives are governed by precept
as no narrative discussed here has been since "The Hermit"
by Parnell. This, too, created difficulties:

> We are, in the main, of your opinion, that Erasmus and
> his letters are tiresome; but then, please [to] recollect that
> we had our moral to work out, and to show, to the satis-
> faction or dissatisfaction of the reader, how in various
> professions young men may get on without patronage.
> To the good of our moral we were obliged to sacrifice;
> perhaps we have sacrificed in vain.[29]

Crabbe was aware of Maria Edgeworth's work, and he was
ambivalent:

> Did you know R. L. Edgeworth? You know the *one* omis-
> sion in all the works of his daughter, and her sentiments
> are said to be derived from him? Were they indeed unbe-
> lievers in revealed religion? It is a questionable point in
> England with those who knew them only in their publica-
> tions. Miss Edgeworth, as a moralist is almost
> unexceptionable—I do not say entirely so; and if she has
> the misfortune to be without the comfort which the Gos-
> pel affords, she has performed a difficult task in preserv-
> ing her morals unconnected with religion. If she believe
> in any sense of the word, even the lowest, I perceive no
> reason for her reserve, since she needed not to have been
> so pointed as to have espoused any of the various de-
> nominations of Christians. Of her general character, I am
> disposed to think highly, and of her writings almost en-
> thusiastically. She has that happy faculty of letting you
> know what she means, so that you do not have to stop
> every little while and say to yourself, "What is all this
> about?"[30]

It is not an easy task to imagine Maria Edgeworth having
difficulty in "preserving her morals," and in the terms "al-

most unexceptionable" and "almost enthusiastically" there
is evident an uneasiness in Crabbe not entirely limited to the
welfare of Maria Edgeworth's immortal soul, for he found a
grating insufficiency in the orderly demonstration of the
Edgeworthian system that conformed so readily to the already existing system of poetic justice. In "The Learned
Boy" (*Tales in Verse*) Crabbe takes typical Edgeworthian material and assumptions and mocks them. The central
character is a not very bright boy who, lacking other virtues,
writes a neat hand, arrives punctually, and works diligently
at his desk in the office. This simple mind, first possessed by
a trifling religiosity, is taken over by an equally foolish
atheism, but during this whole process Stephen Jones remains orderly, even in the acquisition and arrangement of
infidel books:

> The books were view'd, the price was fairly paid,
> And Stephen read, undaunted, undismay'd—
> But not till first he paper'd all the row,
> And placed in order, to enjoy the show;
> Next letter'd all the backs with care and speed,
> Set them in ranks, and then began to read.
>
> (ll. 303–8)[31]

This is a promising beginning for a boy in a tale by Maria
Edgeworth. Crabbe goes on to insist, however, that the
principle of order of the kind Edgeworth advocated was too
simple a proposition for the complexities of life:

> The love of order,—I the thing receive
> From reverend men, and I in part believe—
> Shows a clear mind and clean, and whoso needs
> This love but seldom in the world succeeds;
> And yet with this some other love must be,
> Ere I can fully to the fact agree.
> . . . .
> Still has the love of order found a place
> With all that's low, degrading, mean, and base, ⎫
> With all that merits scorn, and all that meets disgrace:⎬
> In the cold miser, of all change afraid; ⎭

> In pompous men, in public seats obey'd;
> In humble placemen, heralds, solemn drones,
> Fanciers of flowers, and lads like Stephen Jones;
> Order to these is armour and defense,
> And love of method serves in lack of sense.
>
> (ll. 309–27, *passim*)

There are disagreements between Crabbe and Edgeworth, which one must be conscious of before comparing them. Nonetheless, though their opinions about the best end for mankind might have differed, they held much in common: both took their stories from "real life," or tried to make it seem that they did. Where they carried these stories is, of course, a different matter.

Taking Edgeworth's "Rosanna" (1802) as an example, one sees that this long prose tale yields several possible groundworks for tales by Crabbe.[32] I am not saying that Crabbe borrowed these subjects from Edgeworth—on the contrary, but I would say that a tale by Maria Edgeworth separates easily into a number of subjects that Crabbe could have "worked up into something." "Rosanna" is a story about the exemplary family of Farmer Gray; the precise degree of its exemplariness is defined by a number of contrasts afforded by persons in the neighborhood. If one neighbor, O'Doughterty, is honest but not industrious, another neighbor, Hopkins, is dishonest but industrious. The Grays represent the happy instance of the honest and the industrious, and, to be both secure and happy, people in the social class of the Grays ought to take this example to heart. The neighborhood includes other exemplary kinds, who illustrate various home truths. High station assures neither security nor morality: the squire, who is seeking reelection to Parliament, has sold himself to the party in power and lusts after Farmer Gray's daughter and is thereby a rival to his serving-man. Even Farmer Gray's two sons have a brief, atypical moment when they imprudently consider the possibility of enlisting. Hopkins, the middleman, is the kind of subject that would have offered Crabbe an opportunity to construct a narrative about the progress of avarice in a man's mind, a process that Edgeworth does not delineate. In "The Struggles of Conscience," Crabbe builds a story out of a man's dialogue with his conscience over a period of decades, during which time he continues to deceive himself and his conscience about his shady business dealings until, after a particularly reprehensible deed, his conscience is suddenly awakened, resoundingly and permanently. Taking the simple grouping of master, servant, and farm girl in "Rosanna," one can see what Crabbe did with similar material in " 'Squire Thomas," a tale discussed in chapter 3. The two brothers, who in "Rosanna" wisely refrain from going off to war, are similar to a pair to be found in "The Brothers" (*Tales in Verse*). In Crabbe's tale, one brother does go off to sea while the other remains on land to exploit the sailor's generosity, and, after rejecting his impoverished and dying sailor-brother, the landsman ends with the inevitably sterile remorse.[33]

What one sees here is comparable material, not sources; Crabbe carries his stories off in a direction alien to Edgeworth, who plants her standard in the essentially preceptive on behalf of a militant poetic justice. Both work with "real" situations, but one develops these in accord with the "real course of nature" and the other acts on the grounds that vice must be punished and virtue rewarded in terms that self-interest can comprehend.

Jeffrey therefore had a point when he observed that Crabbe's tales could be "ranked by the side of the inimitable tales of Miss Edgeworth." Yet the "weighty and practical precept" of Edgeworth's tales does not determine the conduct of Crabbe's tales. In his attack on Crabbe the reviewer of *The Christian Observer* asks, "Does he instruct us?" No, the reviewer concludes, he really does not, except on a relatively low plane. It is true that his delineations of character are "conducive to the cultivation of that discriminative faculty . . . so useful in our intercourse with mankind"; it is also true that his "inimitable home strokes" help us to judge "our own minds and our own motives"; and of course it is true that he offers "direct satire on some of the most common, and therefore, perhaps, most fatal errors which meet us in our ordinary plans of life. . . ."[34] In short, Crabbe does in his verse tales what Inchbald said the novelist must do, but unfortunately, Crabbe does not elevate either his subjects or his readers above all this, as a poet should. Nor can we read Crabbe and learn how to improve our position in society and still stay happy and decent, as we can when we read Edgeworth's tales. Crabbe, unlike Godwin and Inchbald, does not indict the unjust system of society that creates wicked passions and then punishes us for them, especially if we are poor. Yet, despite these differences, Crabbe as a narrative poet holds more in common with these writers than with any other group of narrative writers.

As analytic as Godwin, often employing a narrative structure, not similar to, but identical with, Inchbald's story of Agnes Primrose, and looking to "real life" for his groundwork, as did the exemplary Maria Edgeworth, Crabbe, the narrative poet, created a new kind of verse tale, marked by his closest affinities. In the larger view, one does not have to look at the verse tale of the eighteenth and early nineteenth centuries to explain the peculiar narrative art of Crabbe; something much closer to him is immediately at hand, the prose fiction that he read every day and that he himself produced during one period of his life. Much has been made of Crabbe's relation to Augustan verse satire, and probably too much cannot be made of it—it is essential to an understanding of Crabbe's poetry, narrative or otherwise. His loyalty to it was, in effect, the origin of his literary troubles; yet the intention of the satirical verse tradition was still active, even in Crabbe's own period, though in another form. Between Crabbe's poetry and the moral epistles of Pope and the satires of Churchill stands the novel. Crabbe's final achievement as a poet is that he adapted the novel to narrative poetry and that, in so doing, he remained faithful to those principles he had accepted on his setting out as a poet.

6

CRABBE'S TALES

Out of Augustan premises, moral theory, an old genre
of satire, and a new form, the novel, and, to a lesser extent,
a once-popular preceptive-progress tale and a still-
adaptable pathetic one, Crabbe produced his verse tales,
subordinating all to a central action of the mind. There are,
it is true, times in his verse tales when the complexity of the
action is greater than any means he has available for representing it; yet the integrity of his action is invariable, vari-
able as may have been his success, various as were the ways
in which he sought to shape it. It is this central interest that,
by dominating his tales, gives them unity, an action irreversible in its progress and often pathetic in its consequences.
It is a mistake, I believe, to see Crabbe's verse tales as the
result of an unconscious or merely fortuitous development
from Augustan satire, from, as it were, the "character" to
the tale, without a conscious intervention on Crabbe's part.
When Crabbe began to write the tales published in *Poems*
and *The Borough*, he was already an experienced writer of
narrative, having produced during the 1790s three novels

and a volume of unpublished verse tales. The four tales that appear at the end of *The Borough* are therefore not new developments; their origins lie far back in Crabbe's career. In a career of nearly six decades, four of these did not pass without Crabbe's working in one way or another with narrative. He early saw it as a solution to his literary problems; he repeatedly returned to it until he had made it a workable solution in fact, and he stayed with it to the end.

His narrative practice reflects his long-held assumptions about the nature and limits of his subject matter and its affective power; his moral and literary universe is the ordinary one of familiar choices, not the less subtle for being widely shared, its consequences radical in their conclusions though gradual in their accumulation. As a priest he distrusted evangelical reliance on sudden infusions of grace to change lives and save souls. Where some saw the spirit, the whole tenor of his writing indicates that he saw pride, fancy, and ignorance. For Crabbe the Anglican priest, as for Crabbe the narrative poet, habitual conduct in daily life determines one's character and ultimate dispensation. I wish here to single out a topic that Crabbe dealt with at length in at least one sermon and in many of his verse tales, the kinds and degrees of wickedness. There are, Crabbe believed, four kinds of sinners: first, those who are "notoriously" wicked, "openly abandoned and given over to evil"; second, those who are "under the dominion . . . of one particular sin but in other respects decent and even praiseworthy"; third, those who "forget God"; fourth, those who are "uncharitable," the law-abiding, the seemingly pious, the merely respectable.[1] These kinds of sinners and their degrees of sinfulness are active, even decisive terms in the tales in *The Borough* and *Tales in Verse*; and Crabbe's turning away from them in *Tales of the Hall* creates his need for a new narrative procedure in representing the turns and movements of heart and mind.

Of the four tales published in *The Borough* only that of Ellen Orford, resigned, suffering, and loving, stands outside Crabbe's classes of sinners—a village saint. The story of Abel Keene is that of the man who forgets God, whereas "Peter Grimes" and "The Parish-Clerk" represent the processes of the habit-ruined, passion-ridden mind in terms of the "notoriously," "openly" wicked man, Grimes, and of a man essentially decent except for the "dominion . . . of one particular sin," Jachin, the parish clerk, who is led by pride and avarice into the habit of the sin that destroys him. As Lilian Haddakin has shown, the clerk's prototype is Sir Balaam of Pope's progress tale in "Epistle to Bathhurst."[2] Only sixty lines long, "Sir Balaam" is the concisely rendered progress of the worldly rise and fall of a merchant whose career illustrates one of the uses of riches. Sir Balaam's frugality yields to an increasing avarice that, in turn, leads to extravagance and dishonesty; worse deeds follow and the merchant dies blaspheming on the gallows. He has been tempted by the devil and has fallen:

> The Tempter saw his time; the work he ply'd;
> Stocks and Subscriptions pour on ev'ry side,
> 'Till all the Daemon makes his full descent,
> In one abundant show'r of Cent. per Cent.,
> Sinks deep within him, and possesses whole,
> Then dubs Director, and secures his soul.
>
> (ll. 369–74)[3]

Crabbe's Jachin shares puritanism with Sir Balaam as well as a love of money, criminality, and something like his unhappy fate. Nevertheless, as Haddakin has observed, Crabbe's treatment of Jachin differs significantly from Pope's treatment of Sir Balaam, for Crabbe "is primarily interested in Jachin's mind" (p. 89), or, as Varley Lang has said, Crabbe transforms the "external" of the Augustans to the "internal," a change that, for Lang, is the "most significant development of Crabbe's realism."[4] Whether Augustan representation of character is as "external" as Lang seems to think is a question, but it is undeniable that Crabbe's representations are many degrees more "internal" than are those of the Augustan satirist. In addition, Crabbe lowers the social level of action and actor in "The Parish-Clerk"; stocks and bonds in Pope's tale become coins in the parish collection plate. Moreover, "The Parish-Clerk" is five times longer than "Sir Balaam," for Crabbe must represent in detail the gradual emergence of sinful habit in a self-righteous man.

A man of austere native disposition and dangerously proud, Jachin, in petty circumstances, desires petty wealth. For all this, he is not a bad man; he is "sober, chaste, devout, and just," a harmless fellow trusted by his neighbors. Crabbe asks, "By what means will pride and avarice deprave a mind of this kind and how will the man's austerity lend itself to crime in gratifying these passions?" In a bad year, with few christenings and weddings, "Desire of gain, with fear of want combined, / Raised sad commotion in his wounded mind . . ." (ll. 138–39).[5] Thus begins Jachin's progress toward theft, the first criminal act being but the initiation of a habit:

> any sin whatever is committed with less reluctance a second time than a first, and is harder to be repented of; it is more willingly yet a third time, than the second . . . and now it begins to be a habit; . . . the struggle of conscience grows fainter and the power of temptation stronger, till the soul is ensnared in the practice, and one sinful action then becomes a habit of sinning. (Crabbe, *Post Sermons,* pp. 56–57)

The poet and sermon-writer were consistent; Crabbe transforms this internal process into narrative progress:

> Oft was he forced his reasons to repeat,
> Ere he could kneel in quiet at his seat;
> But custom soothed him.—Ere a single year
> All this was done without restraint or fear:
> Cool and collected, easy and composed,
> He was correct till all the service closed;

Then to his home, without a groan or sigh,
Gravely he went, and laid his treasure by.
(ll. 213–20)

A habit is now established, and the tale moves to its principal incident, the exposure of Jachin's thefts before the congregation. Crabbe is less interested in the possibilities of the discovery itself than he is in the effects that this event has on Jachin's mind. The passion of shame replaces the passion of pride, as the austere mind turns on itself, and the man suffers and perishes. The progress of the movement from pride and avarice to shame and remorse is completed:

To a lone loft he went, his dying place,
And, as the vicar of his state inquired,
Turn'd to the wall and silently expired!
(ll. 298–300)

Pope achieved in "Sir Balaam" the rapidity of narration that is the essence of the traditional progress tale. Of necessity he simplified the mental processes of his central character and contrived a Satan who tempts and damns and who, as agent of Sir Balaam's fall, is integral to the tale. Crabbe, imitating Pope, has a Satan too, but this Satan is little more than a figure of speech. It is not Satan who tempts and damns Jachin, but Jachin's own passions and his poverty. In Pope's tale Satan offers the bait and Sir Balaam takes it— that is all one knows or needs to know. In "The Parish-Clerk," Crabbe heeds the general direction of Sir Balaam's progress, but the nature of Crabbe's examination of the minute changes in a man's mind produces a shape and texture very different from those of "Sir Balaam." Pope's tale is intended to illustrate an implied maxim; Crabbe's, to reveal how the mind functions under certain external and internal pressures. Pope achieves the narrative rapidity of the progress; Crabbe amplifies the progress in order to register minute changes. "The Parish-Clerk" is closer to the story of Agnes Primrose than it is to its model. This difference arises, in large part, from Crabbe's and Inchbald's subjects, the tragedies of low life and from their attitude toward those subjects, a perceptive sympathy that lays bare the mind and traces the involutions of feeling and habit over a long period of time.

Peter Grimes is one of "the cruel and unjust, who steal and plunder, who habitually lie and deceive, who . . . make all about them . . . wretched and wicked like themselves; these condemn *themselves*, by their evil doings, in the sight of all men . . . " (*Post. Sermons*, p. 57). He is a bad son, a thief, a sadist, a murderer, and a hunted madman. According to a passage from *Marmion*, which Crabbe used as the motto of this tale, he is

> a sordid, soul,
> Such as does murder for a meed;
> Who, but of fear, knows no control,
> Because his conscience, sear'd and foul,
> Feels not the import of the deed;
> One whose brute-feeling ne'er aspires
> Beyond his own more brute desires.

Crabbe's motto stops there, but Scott's poem does not; it continues:

> Such tools the Tempter ever needs,
> To do the savagest of deeds;
> For them no vision'd terrors daunt,
> Their nights no fancied spectres haunt,
> One fear with them, of all most base,
> The fear of death, alone finds place.
>
> (2.22)[6]

For Scott, some men are beyond the reach of any feeling except the fear of death. Crabbe did not agree, and "Peter Grimes" is an instance in support of the other side of the question: there is no man so insensitive as to be incapable of suffering and imagining. The preface to *The Borough* considers the issue at some length:

> The mind here exhibited is one untouched by pity, unstung by remorse, and uncorrected by shame; yet is this hardihood of temper and spirit broken by want, disease, solitude, and disappointment; and he becomes the victim of a distempered and horror-stricken fancy. . . . The ruffian of Mr. *Scott* has a mind of this nature: he has no shame or remorse: but the corrosion of hopeless want, the wasting of unabating disease, and the gloom of unvaried solitude, will have their effect on every nature; and, the harder that nature is, and the longer time required to work upon it, so much the more strong and indelible is the impression.[7]

Crabbe, having selected the most difficult case of all, the "flinty" and "depraved" mind, makes the breakdown of that mind under external and internal pressures the action of the tale. In the first part of "Peter Grimes" Crabbe delineates the progressive hardening of Grimes's mind, as he moves from a "stubborn boy" to a petty thief; time passes, and the severity of his crimes increases as does his passion for power and cruelty:

> He wanted some obedient boy to stand
> And bear the blow of his outrageous hand;
> And hoped to find in some propitious hour
> A feeling creature subject to his power.
>
> (ll. 55–58)[8]

An apprentice is found, tormented, and then mysteriously dies; another boy replaces him, and he too dies. A third boy comes, and dies: "The pitying women raised a clamour round, / And weeping said, 'Thou hast thy 'prentice drown'd' " (ll. 153–54).

Not punished by the law but ostracized by the community, Grimes now exists in complete isolation; the second part of the tale begins with the representation of the forces that are driving him mad:

> Thus by himself compell'd to live each day,
> To wait for certain hours the tide's delay;
> At the same times the same dull views to see,
> The bounding marsh-bank and the blighted tree;
> . . . .
> There anchoring, Peter chose from man to hide,
> There hang his head, and view the lazy tide
> In its hot slimy channel slowly glide.
>
> (ll. 171–87, *passim*)

Isolation having done its work, his mind is as blighted as the place in which he lives, "Where all presented to the eye or ear / Oppress'd the soul with misery, grief, and fear" (ll. 203–4). Now disease and nightmares take over—"Wild were his dreams, and oft he rose in fright, / Waked by his view of horrors in the night—" (ll. 225–26). Grief and terror replace obduracy and dullness. A year passes, and Peter Grimes has become a regular feature of the landscape:

> Of sea-fowl swimming by no heed he took,
> But on the gliding waves still fix'd his lazy look;
> At certain stations he would view the stream,
> As if he stood bewilder'd in a dream.
>
> (ll. 241–44)

But when men seek him out, in pity or curiosity, he breaks down and flees in terror; dying, he is captured and carried to the parish poor house. The third part of the tale is the account of Grimes's hallucinations and death.

This is the tale's principal incident, one that is largely declamatory, but Grimes's monologue is complex, for rationalizations, cunning, and self-pity intermix as declaimed description makes external and visible what was internal and hidden. All that had transfixed Grimes in the second part of the tale is now presented to the reader:

"—I fixed my eyes
"On the mid stream and saw the spirits rise;
"I saw my father on the water stand,
"And hold a thin pale boy in either hand;
. . . .
"And 'Come,' they said, with weak, sad voices, 'come.'
"To row away with all my strength I try'd;
"But there were they, hard by me in the tide,
"The three unbodied forms—and 'Come,' still 'come,' they
    cried."

(ll. 306–24, *passim*)

" 'Again, they come,' and mutter'd as he died" (l. 375); so
Grimes dies, demonstrating that no mind is impervious to
the interaction of the powers of external and internal
worlds.

Description of setting is pervasively and functionally
present in "Peter Grimes," but Crabbe does not describe
merely for the sake of describing, as Scott does in *Marmion*.
The landscape in this tale is one of the forces affecting
Grimes's mind; its blight is an analogue of his state of mind
as well as the reality out of which rise his hallucinatory
visions. The reader sees the landscape that Grimes sees,
then sees Grimes as an isolated figure in that scene, and
finally sees in the dying man's mind the unreal phantoms in
the real world. In no other tale of Crabbe's will one find so
sophisticated and economical use of point of view, nor in
the scenic disposition of the fable so complex a structure.

Scott is a descriptive poet who wanted to paint landscapes
and some of the more picturesque of human attitudes and
situations—a knight in a castle, a nun in a convent, a king
with his mistress. Crabbe is analytic, concerned with interesting moments only insofar as they represent or affect a
mental and moral process. Scott evaded a problem by
merely asserting that a certain character was incapable of
any significant response; but Crabbe, and it is greatly to his
credit, created a narrative action out of the intractability of
that character's mind. He subdued landscape to his narra-

tive purpose, making it at once an extension of consciousness and, in part, a cause of changes within that mind; it is a
scene and an agent, but never, as it was with *Marmion*, the
groundwork of an action. The groundwork of Crabbe's tale
is the slow collapse of a hardened mind, and Crabbe has
forced new complications upon the reader by making him
pity first Grimes's victims and then Grimes himself. Passion
is being worked upon—the reader must sympathize with
the most difficult case of all—but the occasion is "real" and
Crabbe intends that one respond, not to high ornament and
exclamation, but to the complexities of the mind and the
sufferings of our kind. In this way, Crabbe deepened and
intensified the emotional force of the representation of
mind and manners.

"Peter Grimes" and "The Parish-Clerk" are more pre-
dominantly descriptive in method and thus more scenic in
their organization than are the tales Crabbe published in
Tales in Verse in 1812, two years after *The Borough* appeared.
In *Tales in Verse* Crabbe drastically foreshortens scene in
deference to process. "Peter Grimes" and "The Parish
Clerk" are tales about notorious wickedness or a dominant
sin subject to the punishment of the law. Most of the tales in
Tales in Verse have to do with the uncharitable, who break no
laws and are not exposed to the community's wrath, but
who belong among the wicked nonetheless.

> The uncharitable, therefore, must be reckoned among
> the wicked. These are hard-hearted, cruel, selfish, and
> unkind . . . they may not transgress any positive law of
> man, or obtain any grievous evil report, yet they are in
> the number of the wicked, and rebel against the repeated
> commandment of their God . . . they become almost the
> enemies of mankind; they are tyrants and torments in
> their families, uncourteous to their superiors, unpitiful to
> those below them, and unfriendly with all around them.
> (*Post. Sermons*, p. 57)

The subjects in *Tales in Verse* are as ordinary and as shape-
less as daily life; with them, Crabbe creates a verse narrative

stripped of all circumstances but those essential to a representation of a mental process. He does not wish to elevate his subjects, for that would falsify them, or his readers, because he does not believe that is necessary or possible. His intention, rather, is to define within the narrowest bounds the movements of the mind, to delineate the daily process whereby passions grow, habits arise, and character gradually changes.

In "Procrastination," one of the better known tales in *Tales in Verse*, one can watch Crabbe working within these rigorous and self-imposed limitations. This is the tale of "kind" Rupert and "prudent" Dinah, and in these epithets lies the essential contrast that is finally dramatized in the tale's principal incident. The action of "Procrastination" is the death of love, specifically, how in Dinah's mind the passion of avarice slowly supplants the passion of love and how avarice, in turn, is transformed into the passion of pride. The fable begins with the young lovers, plighted but poor, and ends with the wealthy, middle-aged woman snubbing her impoverished former lover, the kind Rupert. The narrative base of this poem is the gradually accumulating minutes, hours, and seasons in which the circumstances of daily life play upon and direct the passions that agitate and change the mind. The principal method of composition is contrast, a contrast of before and after, of dispositions of the mind, and of destinies. Summary covers the work of the years in the manner of a progress, and in the principal incident declamation and description bring to eye and heart the consequences of the mind's gradual processes.

Marriage is delayed while Rupert goes abroad to acquire the necessary money; Dinah remains in the household of her aunt and learns to value the charms of wealth:

> This hope, these comforts cherish'd day by day,
> To Dinah's bosom made a gradual way;
> Till love of treasure had as large a part
> As love of Rupert in the virgin's heart.
> . . . .

> Now the grave niece partook the widow's cares;
> Look'd to the great, and ruled the small affairs;
> Saw clean'd the plate, arranged the china show,
> And felt her passion for a shilling grow.
> . . . .
> This passion grew, and gain'd at length such sway,
> That other passions shrank to make it way;
> Romantic notions now the heart forsook.
>
> (ll. 80–102, *passim*)[9]

In time, Dinah becomes a rich woman, inheriting her aunt's "love of hoarding and her dread of waste." Dinah is still in the relatively early stages of her habit of uncharitableness, but as the seasons pass she smugly grows harder:

> She knew that mothers grieved, and widows wept,
> And she was sorry, said her prayers, and slept.
> Thus pass'd the seasons, and to Dinah's board
> Gave what the seasons to the rich afford.
>
> (ll. 140–43)

A "love of splendour" contends with avarice and slowly overcomes it, for Dinah now takes pride in the display of her wealth:

> Above her head, all gorgeous to behold,
> A time-piece stood on feet of burnish'd gold;
> A stag's-head crest adorn'd the pictured case,
> Through the pure crystal shown th'enamell'd face;
> And, while on brilliants moved the hands of steel,
> It click'd from pray'r to pray'r, from meal to meal.
>
> (ll. 174–79)

It is in a room ostentatiously filled with objects like this that Dinah is seated when, after years of absence and failure, Rupert suddenly returns, and the principal incident is underway. In Dinah the years of "deliberation, reasoning, resolution, willing, consenting"[10] have done their work, and her prudent disposition, abetted by the accidents of her life,

is now hardened in its pride. She will not have this broken
and rough man whom she once loved. He, as declamation
makes clear, at first does not understand what has happened, then is astonished, and finally is enraged:

"Speak, then, my fate; for these my sorrows past,
"Time lost, youth fled, hope wearied, and at last
"This doubt of thee—a childish thing to tell,
"But certain truth—my very throat they swell;
"They stop the breath, and but for shame could I
"Give way to weakness, and with passion cry;
"These are unmanly struggles. . . ."

(ll. 279–85)

Passionate declamation is throttled by natural behavior,
passionately described by the sufferer. As for Dinah: "His
soul she loved, and hoped he had the grace / To fix his
thoughts upon a better place" (ll. 289–90). Crabbe, in the
manner of Inchbald, sketches a few telling circumstances
intended to convey the intensity of the passions at work and
to carry the action to its conclusion, the end of love and
hope: "He her small fingers moulded in his hard / And
bronzed broad hand; then told her, his regard / His best
respect were gone. . ."(ll. 293–95).

Out of the principal incident come consequences that
provide the powerful conclusion to this tale. The aging
man, sick and poor, is forced to accept the charity of the
parish, and, so circumstanced, provides the necessary
contrast to the thriving Dinah with his "plain artless look"
and her "sharp meaning face":

It might some wonder in a stranger move,
How these together could have talk'd of love.

(ll. 317–18)

Crabbe relies on the same radical contrast that Inchbald
employed when Agnes Primrose confronted her seducer in
her judge. The present seems to make the past impossible,

but, of course, what the contrast actually implies is all that the operations of the mind and the real tendency of things can effect over a long time. There is a reversal for these lovers, but it is not the sudden and felicitous one of the eighteenth-century pathetic tale, for this reversal is the work of years, and the wicked flourish while the virtuous suffer. Again, in the final incident of the story Crabbe, insisting on contrast, brings his narrative to a complex instant in which all the motions of Dinah's mind, old and new, are set to work, an instant that culminates in the most petty but cutting of snubs:

> But Dinah moves—she had observed before
> The pensive Rupert at an humble door.
> Some thoughts of pity raised by his distress,
> Some feeling touch of ancient tenderness;
> Religion, duty, urged the maid to speak
> In terms of kindness to a man so weak;
> But pride forbad, and to return would prove
> She felt the shame of his neglected love;
> Nor wrapp'd in silence could she pass, afraid
> Each eye should see her, and each heart upbraid.
> One way remain'd—the way the Levite took,
> Who without mercy could on misery look,
> (A way perceived by craft, approv'd by pride):
> She cross'd, and pass'd him on the other side.
>
> (ll. 336–49)

With this the tale ends. Dinah belongs now among the wicked. Her affront is the sign of a complexly felt but irreversible hardening of the heart. Crabbe has represented how, in the circumstances of a well-ordered, seemingly pious daily life, the mind of a sinner grew harder as each snug day continued to gratify passions and thus helped to form ineradicable habits. The next time Dinah meets Rupert on the street of their town, she will feel less uneasy, and at last she will feel nothing at all.

"The Convert," from *Tales in Verse*, is a progress tale

about another category of sinner, the man who has forgotten God.[11] The story of John Dighton is the story of his two conversions, the first to a rigid dissenting sect and the second to the popularized skepticism of political radicalism, which are but stages in his progress toward absolute despair. In the first part of the tale, John Dighton is an active, intelligent, but not always too scrupulous cast-off child growing up in the worst kind of poverty. In the second part, Dighton, now a young man, responding to the passion of fear, converts—and it is a genuine conversion—to the faith of the dissenting meetinghouse; with religious certainty comes stability, and Dighton starts a family and begins to thrive in a small stationer's shop. In the third and longest part, Crabbe traces the progress of Dighton's unhappy mind in the midst of his increasing wealth and his growing intellectual presumption. Passionately John Dighton now rejects the brethren and as passionately embraces the skepticism advocated in the books he sells. His conversion to philosophy is as unreasoned as was his conversion to religion. A self-educated and a half-educated man, the wealthy John Dighton doubts everything, despairs, and dies. His tale is the progress from a boy's poverty and dissipation to a young man's religiosity and prosperity, and finally to meaningless wealth, godlessness, and lasting sorrow. By now a familiar figure, Dighton was a relatively new figure in narrative, a mind that founders on reason, led to disaster by passions that the man does not recognize in himself. This progress is appropriately sparing of narrative detail and is interrupted only at most critical points by declamations. Its primary method is summary, summary of the mind's changes as it is modified by passions, which are the source of all John Dighton's actions and reactions.

The "Unhappy Dighton" dies, unhappy and unlucky, too, for here was a man with a good native disposition, who, owing to the accidents of his life, never encountered the friend who would have revealed to him the rational grounds of hope and fear, the "proper place of reason" and virtue, the necessary companion of grace. Falling into the hands of well-intentioned dissenters, who relied solely on emotion, and then coming under the influence of skeptical books, Dighton could find no adequate explanation for his life. Fear led to pride, and pride to doubt, and doubt and sadness accompanied him to his end. Crabbe represents in "The Convert" a moral tragedy overtaking and ruining a mind and a life, the isolated and uninstructed mind of a rising class left without the traditional support of faith with reason.

Although "The Patron" and "Edward Shore" rely more on incident and description than does "The Convert," both of these tales from *Tales in Verse* are similar to Dighton's story; they too trace the progress of passion in the ruined mind. The sensitive poet in "The Patron" has a mind that is in its weakness susceptible to the illusions of hope and, when the time comes, is unable to withstand the real griefs that follow unreal hopes.[12] Edward Shore's mind, on the other hand, progressively degenerates because it is too vigorous. Doubting like John Dighton, and doubting arrogantly, Shore does not have the necessary moral strength, which religious principles would have given him, to withstand an adulterous passion. He, like Jachin, falls, and feels "in full force the censure and the crime" (1.308), but in trying to forget what he has done, Shore turns to "his fierce passions and his daring pride" (l. 333), and these drive him into new vices; poverty and imaginary terrors assail him as they did Peter Grimes and drive him to "despair and anguish . . . / The wreck and ruin of a noble mind" (ll. 390–91).[13]

In all of Crabbe's tales in *Tales in Verse*, whether painful or comic, the operations of the mind are the central action. In the fablelike story "The Struggles of Conscience" Crabbe represents the lifelong relationship of a man and his conscience. Quiet when he is good, chiding when he ventures on dishonesty for avarice's sake, the conscience takes its vengeance when he commits an unforgivable sin against another person. Like Shore, he seeks to obliterate what he

has done in dissipation, but this man, now among the
wicked, sees only his sin in whatever he looks at. Like
Grimes, he finds his days and nights a horror:

> Such was his life—no other changes came,
> The hurrying day, the conscious night the same;
> The night of horror—when he, starting, cried
> To the poor startled sinner at his side:
> "Is it the law? am I condemned to die?"
>
> (ll. 480–84)[14]

In a comic tale, "The Gentleman Farmer," the story of a
weak mind ruled by pride, Crabbe represents the process
whereby a clever woman, a cynical doctor, and a hypocriti-
cal dissenting preacher all play upon this passion and control the gentleman-farmer's mind.[15] In "Arabella," another
comic tale, Crabbe shows how even the mind of a bluestock-
ing can adjust itself to almost any thing, if enough time has
elapsed. The young Arabella breaks off a match when she
learns that her fiancé has fathered a bastard; but the
middle-aged Arabella is less fastidious: when she learns that
her new husband-to-be has a separate establishment and a
large and growing family of illegitimate children, she finds
within herself plausible reasons for going ahead with the
marriage.[16] "The Wager" is probably the most "plotted" of
the tales in this collection and certainly the one with the
shortest period of time allotted for its action; still, even
within these limitations, Crabbe manages to demonstrate
how the weak but obstinate mind of a clinging woman can,
by playing upon the passions of her husband, dominate his
life.[17] "The Parting Hour" and "Resentment" delineate the
gradual waste of life and joy in an action that encompasses
decades. "The Parting Hour" is the story of the slow decay
of mind and strength and the attrition in time of all love
save charitable love in the real world of accident, separation, and loss.[18] The action of "Resentment" is the growth of
the passion of resentment over a period of years until finally

it has ruined an otherwise good and charitable mind; it concludes with charity extended too late and offers its leading character only years of inextinguishable remorse.[19]

In these tales as well as in those which have been examined more closely, Crabbe tried within the limits of only a few hundred lines to encompass a lifetime in which passions continually operate on a mind and to assess the consequences of these processes. Foreshortening these processes in summary and dramatizing their consequences in the principal incident of his tales, Crabbe brought over into verse narrative the materials and the purposes of the radical novelists. Like them, he was interested essentially in the internal operations of the mind, and, like them, he was interested in the relation of inner events to the accidents of the external world. There is another dimension to Crabbe's narrative art: the action of his tales implies and reflects the effects of external events. Had Jachin not known unusually harsh poverty in a difficult year, he probably never would have become a thief. Had Rupert not gone abroad, had Dinah's aunt been a different kind of woman, Dinah probably would have been prudent and happy rather than avaricious and proud. Had Dighton been born into a settled family and into the established church, he would have been the same active, intelligent man but not the doubt-ridden sinner who forgot God. Had Edward Shore's intellectual energy not expended itself too often on radical works, his religious principles probably would have withstood the test of sexual passion. Had the sensitive poet not been casually taken up and as casually cast aside by a noble patron, he probably would never have formed his deadly hopes. Peter Grimes remains the only figure in these tales whose evil is beyond the effect of accident, and yet even he feels the terrible force of his external conditions. Crabbe's tales, then, are not to be separated from the external world, weighty as their emphasis is upon internal processes. Whether passions make men fools or villains, ridiculous or pitiful, they nonetheless arise from the interaction of the intrinsic nature of man with the forces of the real world. Out of this principle Crabbe contrived the tales in *The Borough* and *Tales in Verse*; it determined his central action, his interest in ordinary life, his realism, his technique. He shares it with the radical novelists, whose political principles he rejected but whose narrative method is his own.

In *Tales of the Hall* (1819), the last work Crabbe saw through the press, he was dealing with essentially the same material of his earlier tales, with essentially the same principles, and with essentially the same prevailing intentions:

> Come, then, fair Truth! and let me clearly see
> The mind I paint, as they are seen in thee;
> To me their merits and their faults impart;
> Give me to say, "frail being! such thou art,"
> And closely let me view the naked human heart.
>
> (ll. 121–25)[20]

Thus even with an elaborate, unsuccessful narrative frame—the story of the reunion of two long-separated brothers and their growing friendship—*Tales of the Hall* is well within the usual bounds of Crabbe's poetry, as he had defined it earlier in *The Borough*:

> 'Tis good to know, 'tis pleasant to impart,
> These turns and movements of the human heart;
> The stronger features of the soul to paint,
> And make distinct the latent and the faint;
> Man, as he is, to place in all men's view.
>
> (ll. 436–40)[21]

Though the purposes and the material remain much the same, important differences distinguish *Tales of the Hall* from Crabbe's earlier tales. For one thing, the tales are now on the average nearly twice as long as those published in 1812; this is more than an old man's loquacity, for in *Tales of the Hall* Crabbe is attempting, with varying degrees of success, to represent the action of the mind in terms even more

elusive and subtle than he had so far done. He readjusted
his narrative method accordingly, elaborating where
hitherto he had concentrated, developing in incident what
he had previously summarized, shifting the principal inci
dent away from its largely pathetic base, whereas before he
had used contrast and declamation to intensify pathos.

Generally, in *Tales of the Hall* Crabbe's treatment of
events, both internal and external, is fuller, and incident
becomes not merely the culmination of the tale, but a basic
unit in its structure that grows out of, and is connected by
summary with other incidents. His stories remain progres
ses of the mind, but the progress is now rendered as a series
of incidents, not as a series of summarized events, or quasi
incidents. The structural and emotional primacy of the
principal incident is diminished. In *Tales of the Hall* this
incident is no longer the only fully realized incident, or one
of the few, as in *Tales in Verse*. Now it is one of a series of its
kind, often the last, certainly the decisive one. The word
decisive is important, for the incident that now is principal is
so, not because it is the emotional consequence of a long
history of passions and habits, but because it is the incident
in which the leading character makes a choice that determines the rest of his life. Ethos, in other words, mixes with
pathos in the principal incident in *Tales of the Hall*, and
impassioned utterance heightens but does not dominate the
incident.

In *Tales of the Hall* Crabbe still concerns himself with
internal mental process, but in this collection he concentrates on a decisive period in a lifetime that leads to an
irrevocable decision. Crabbe asks: How can we, knowing
what we know, make choices so mysteriously wrong? Why
even unwillingly, do we consent to a recognizably wrong
course of action? The answer lies in our native frailty, but
frail as we are, we remain in Crabbe's view complicated and
supersubtle agents. In *Tales in Verse* Crabbe delineated a
process whereby a passion became a prevailing habit, a process that interacted with the accidents of the external world

and worked in accord with the real tendencies of things. He focused on one character's life history, and, out of the contrasts afforded by the consequence of that and another life story, he produced the essential effect of the principal incident; other characters contributed their share to the process that led to this result but, in narrative terms, they were more an occasion for summary than for incident. In *Tales of the Hall* the problem is more complex in both narrative and moral terms. First, in these tales there is the character who, at a given moment, must at last choose; at work within him at this critical instant are his native disposition, his propensities, secret passions, and hidden wishes, many of which he does not consciously acknowledge as his and in his calmer, more rational hours would repudiate. In addition, this choice is made under powerful pressures exerted by other characters, with their own passions and private wishes driving them. Working upon his passions with their own, these other agents contribute to the complexity of the moment within which the decision is made. The internal action of the central character does not become less important, but other characters in these later tales become more important; they cannot be assimilated by summary but must assert themselves in incident, and so the leading characters in these tales congregate around incident and reveal themselves in speech and gesture. Crabbe's tales necessarily become longer.

There is another notable characteristic shared by almost every tale in this collection, the subject of love in all its phases—love rejected, accepted, forgotten, neglected, revived, exploited, betrayed. The old bachelors and old maids, husbands and wives, widows and widowers, abandoned girls, cuckolded husbands, or disappointed lovers—the cast of characters in the eighteenth century's preceptive tale—all have been in love. In fact, in *Tales of the Hall* Crabbe's concern with sex appears at times obsessive. His wife, who had been insane for many years, had died and Crabbe was suddenly released into celebrity and society; now an old man, he found himself attracted by, and attractive to, a number of young women. There were two rash, brief engagements.[22] Hazardous as literary biography is, I shall suggest, nonetheless, that an old man's briefly renewed sexuality brought subtle motions in his own heart to his attention and thus helped to bring about a new approach to long-considered subject matter.

There are two kinds of tales in *Tales of the Hall*, laterally developed narratives, often autobiographical in mode, that begin in youth and continue, incident by incident, into middle or old age. These, the more garrulous and the least structurally complex of the tales, include "The Maid's Story," "The Old Bachelor," "William Bailey," "The Widow's Tale." Their relation to the progress tale is discernible. There is another kind of tale in this collection, one whose action is relatively brief in duration, limited, as in "Delay Has Danger" and "Gretna Green," to a few weeks out of a lifetime. Crabbe narrows the time of the action in tales like these in order to analyze more minutely than before the subtle motions of the minds of his several characters.

"Delay Has Danger," the tale of how a young man comes to marry one girl rather than another, concentrates on a few weeks in the life of Henry, who, affianced to Cecilia, ends by marrying Fanny. There are three minds in this tale, and their interaction is the essence of the tale. There is the firm mind of Cecilia, the girl Henry is supposed to marry and wants to marry; there is Fanny's mind, fond, timid, shallow, commonplace—the girl he does not want to but does marry; then there is Henry's mind, weak and vacillating. His rational choice is Cecilia, but his reason is undercut by the secret promptings of vanity and his will is corrupted by undefined wishes and by his growing fear and shame, the consequences of his failure to tell one girl that he is already engaged to another. Despising and consoling himself alternately, he lets the days pass without acting, and, with each passing day, action becomes more difficult. Fanny does not arouse in this weak man any strong passion, but her evident fondness inspires an ephemeral desire in him, one that undermines rather than overwhelms his judgment; yet he ends by marrying this girl.

Lost in the pleasure of gratified vanity, Henry is aware of Fanny's hopes:

> O! yes, he saw, and he resolved to fly,
> And blamed his heart, unwilling to comply:
> . . . .
> 'Tis thus our secret passions work their way,
> And the poor victims know not they obey.
>
> (ll. 360–71, passim)[23]

He looks to chance to free him from this entanglement, which he could effect himself "could he command the will" (l. 406):

> It was his purpose, every morn he rose,
> The dangerous friendship he had made to close;
> It was his torment nightly, ere he slept,
> To feel his prudent purpose was not kept.
>
> (ll. 432–35)

With the principal incident comes the decision that marks all the narratives of *Tales of the Hall*. Another letter from Cecilia arrives—the last, she warns him, an ultimatum demanding that he return to her and abandon the flirtation with Fanny. His response is as rash as her fierce letter. He thinks of Fanny:

> "I know not what, dear maid!—if thy soft smiles were here."
> And then, that instant, there appear'd the maid,
> . . . .
> In that weak moment, when disdain and pride,
> And fear and fondness, drew the man aside,
> In this weak moment—"Wilt thou," he began,
> "Be mine?" and joy o'er all her features ran;

> "I will!" she softly whisper'd; but the roar
> Of cannon would not strike his spirit more.
>
> (ll. 683–93)

The next day, he awakens to a world as sad and as dejected as he is. He marries Fanny to become "the most repining of repenting men; / With a fond, teasing, anxious wife" (ll. 734–35). Self-love yields to self-contempt. The tale ends, not without its precept, if you wish to call it that:

> Thus will it be when man permits a vice
> First to invade his heart, and then entice;
> When wishes vain and undefined arise,
> And that weak heart, deceive, seduce, surprise;
> When evil Fortune works on Folly's side,
> And rash Resentment adds a spur to Pride;
> Then life's long troubles from these actions come,
> In which a moment may decide our doom.
>
> (ll. 786–93)

In "Delay Has Danger" Crabbe made it clear that both will and reason must guard against vain and undefined wishes in the heart, perpetually subject to sudden, transient passions and chances. The real tendency of things does not tolerate such wishes, which are, in the end, no more than flattering fantasies. Crabbe's characters live in a universe in which they cannot safely indulge themselves. "The Maid's Story" and "Lady Barbara" afford instances of Crabbe's point. The first of these is a tale autobiographical in mode, more than 1,000 lines in length, an elderly spinster's story, beginning in girlhood and continuing to middle age, the account of hopes and fears, losses and disappointments, deeply felt but rationally endured. The principal incident of the tale arises from the courtship of this woman, now middle aged, by an infatuated boy newly out of school, who wants to marry her. She rejects him, of course, describing to him what, in time, their marriage would be:

"Add twenty years to my precarious life,
"And lo! your aged, feeble, wailing wife;
"Displeased, displeasing, discontented, blamed;
"Both, and with cause, shaming and ashamed."

(ll. 1040–43)[24]

'erfectly aware of what such a match would be, she is also
.ware that her refusal must be made in terms so absolute
hat the boy will never again raise the question:

"Did his distress, his pains, your joy excite?—"
No; but I fear'd his perseverance might.
Was there no danger in the moon's soft rays,
To hear the handsome stripling's earnest praise?
Was there no fear that while my words reproved
The eager youth, I might myself be moved?
Not for his sake alone I cried, "persist
No more," and with a frown the cause dismiss'd.

(ll. 1067–74)

he spinster recognizes her frailty, her vulnerability in an
npredictable moment to accident, suggestion, and
nomentary passion. She tolerates no postponements, no
quivocations; her whole history of loss and disappointment
as been, in effect, a preparation for this moment: reason
an see and will can execute. What reason sees is a grim
uture and the mind's susceptibility to its elusive, secret mo-
ions. She passes the test but wills not to have it repeated.

Lady Barbara, in "Lady Barbara; or, the Ghost," does not
ass the test. She, a middle-aged widow, marries a boy
vhom she has known since he was a child and whom she
egards as a son. Like the spinster, she sees clearly what will
ome of this marriage, but, when the moment comes, it is
er own wavering thoughts and the powerful pressure
xerted by the boy's desire that overcome her judgment and
lisable her will. This is instant in which a choice must be
nade, and she consents to the wrong one:

> "O! leave me, I entreat;
> "Leave me a moment—we shall quickly meet."—
> "No! here I kneel, a beggar at thy feet."—
> He said, and knelt—with accents, softer still,
> He woo'd the weakness of a failing will,
> And erring judgment—took her hand, and cried,
> "Withdraw it not!— . . ."
> . . . .
> ——He saw her looks express'd
> Favour and grace—the hand was firmer press'd—
> Signs of opposing fear no more were shown;
> And, as he press'd, he felt it was his own.
>
> (ll. 886–98)

Years later, after a married life of brutal humiliation, Lad
Barbara, now an old woman, looks back on that moment

> "I sinn'd with warning—when I gave my hand,
> "A power within said, urgently—Withstand!
> "And I resisted—O! my God! what shame,
> "What years of torment from that frailty came.
> "That husband-son! . . ."
>
> (ll. 923–27

In these three tales, two of them encompassing decades an
one limited essentially to only a few weeks, the principa
incident involves an instant's choice; what Crabbe discern
there is the danger of reason's being perverted by equivoca
tion, deceived by fantasy, and briefly extinguished by trans
ient passion. Henry and Lady Barbara consent rather tha
will, but the rational spinster actively wills and wills not to b
tempted again.

"Gretna Green" is the story of how a rich young lou
Bellwood, came to be unhappily married and how Dr. Sid
mere, his father-in-law, brought misery on himself and hi
daughter by surreptitiously encouraging this marriage
Moreover, it is a story from "real life," the occasion bein
the elopement of Dr. Samuel Parr's daughter with a ric
young man, her inferior in intellect and cultivation.[26] Th

action of the tale is the action of Dr. Sidmere's equivocating mind as it spins delusions that will wreck lives. His passion is his dignity, and, to him, riches are desirable only as a means of embellishing this dignity. When Mrs. Sidmere suggests in the first incident that Bellwood has taken a fancy to their daughter, Dr. Sidmere finds himself hoping silently but intensely that this marriage will take place. His wife's suggestion has tempted him, and he has fallen. Absorbed in vain wishes, the Sidmeres advance on the implacable and contemptible Bellwood. Dr. Sidmere sees himself as the adviser and ruler of an innocent and affluent young couple, his dignity enhanced by their wealth. Yet his situation is trying; he desires the elopement, but he does not want it to seem that he is permitting a clandestine courtship. While hoping for everything, he can only pretend that he has noticed nothing. Victimized by desire and shame, he must seem not to desire—not even to notice—what he most desires. Still, there are compensations, fantasies of how he will conduct himself after the marriage:

> "Suppose them wed," said he, "and at my feet,
> "I must exclaim that instant—'Vile deceit!'
> . . . .
> "At last, but slowly, I may all forgive,
> "And their adviser and director live."
>
> (ll. 247–52)[27]

Heaven, in its justice, grants Dr. Sidmere his wish: Clara and Bellwood elope. In a series of incidents and summaries—the progress of a marriage—Crabbe represents the rapid collapse of this union as Bellwood grows violent, avaricious, and tyrannical. Three weeks pass, but no trembling young couple approach Dr. Sidmere for forgiveness and advice. Even so, the pleasures of imagination remain. Dr. Sidmere supposes that the bride and groom do not come home because they are afraid; he begins to daydream: "Suppose me there—suppose the carriage stops: / Down on her knees my trembling daughter drops; / Slowly I raise her, in my arms . . ." (ll. 339–441). He then journeys, uninvited, to Bellwood's house only to confront a ghastly reality. In the principal incident his daughter tells him what marriage to Bellwood is: "He made the house a hell that he should share . . ." (l. 384). Were Bellwood only a fool, she would govern him; were he only a brute, she would make "the brute-affection" yield her power; but he is both silly and savage (ll. 387–99, *passim*). Dr. Sidmere advises patience. The daughter's reply is decisive:

> "I am a child no more,
> "Nor more dependent; but, at woman's age,
> "I feel the wrongs provoke me and enrage.
> "Sir, could you bring me comfort, I were cool;
> "But keep your counsel for your boys at school."
> (ll. 406–10)

After this incident there is only summary of growing domestic hatred until at last Bellwood and his wife separate; he lives on, hoping that she will be indiscreet, and she, with a small settlement, takes to "an hired lodging and a widow'd bed" (l. 445). Dr. Sidmere suffers more than either, "His error greater, and his motive less"; nor can he be sure that he "can hide the suffering" he endures (ll. 451–57, *passim*). Dr. Sidmere, like Jachin, has been tempted and has fallen, but Jachin's subsequent conduct demonstrates how habit hardens one to sin. In Dr. Sidmere, we see, instead, the dangerous vitality of vain wishes, which overtake him in a moment's temptation and which he indulges in spite of reason. Crabbe closely observes the workings of his mind as it wavers between daydreams and self-reproach until at last, in a decisive interview with his daughter, he has only self-reproach left, a misery complicated by his fear that men may guess that the great Dr. Sidmere abetted this wretched marriage.

At the opening of this chapter I observed that the kinds and degrees of sins were important categories in *The Borough* and *Tales in Verse*. Those tales dealt with either the decent man subjected to one dominant sin, or the notoriously wicked man, or the uncharitable man, or the man who forgot God. The tales in *Tales of the Hall* do not lend themselves to these categories. The spinster clearly does not sin, but, then, Henry and Lady Barbara err rather than sin, and Dr. Sidmere sins by insidious omission rather than by frank commission. Most of the leading characters in *Tales of the Hall* are not uncharitable, nor notoriously wicked, nor even godless, nor under the domination of one sin; like the hero of "Delay Has Danger," they destroy themselves by succumbing in weak moments to irrevocably wrong choices:

> "Frail was the hero of my tale, but still
> "Was rather drawn by accident than will.
> "Some without meaning into guilt advance,
> "From want of guard, from vanity, from chance."
>
> (ll. 35–38)

After looking closely at the "naked heart," Crabbe saw a phenomenon too complex for him to judge, and in *Tales of the Hall* the action that he represents is so elusive that he no longer attempts to classify it.

"To prevent false hopes . . . ," Crabbe wrote, "when you come to die—to prevent tears and despair also, and what, if possible, is worse than either, to prevent a cold, dead, miserable heart, think seriously, repent truly, and lead a new, holy, and obedient life . . ." (*Post. Sermons*, pp. 66–67). When Crabbe held the mirror of his work before his reader, he particularly would warn the reader of the dead heart. In Crabbe's tales, it is the cold, dead heart that kills, not the cloaked assassin of Gothic fiction or the destructive social system of Godwin's and Inchbald's novels. Sins and some sinners may be categorized, but it was God's task, not Crabbe's, to sort out—among the varieties of complications and extenuations, of sufferings inflicted and endured—the damned from the saved. With the circumspection of his tradition, Crabbe stopped short at the confines of this world and let the sublime poets ascend to things divine; as for heaven and hell, Crabbe approached them, when he did at all, as the projections of dreams or hallucinations. In his tales he viewed the characters and their actions and reactions in the light of revealed religion, but he painted this world as it is, and in preferring the hope of divine justice in the next world to poetic justice in this, he also preferred not to speak overmuch of the former in the secular realm of his tales.

The tales in *The Borough* and *Tales in Verse* look to the prose fiction of Godwin, Inchbald, and Edgeworth; it may also be said that *Tales of the Hall* looks toward a kind of prose fiction that had not yet been written—I am referring to the novels of George Eliot, those monuments of sympathetic analysis, and to the choices made in critical instants by Bullstrode, Tito, Gwendolen Hartleth, and Arthur Donnithorne. In Crabbe's tales, the action is never reversible; in his earlier tales passions lead to habits and habits are fixed and fixing. In *Tales of the Hall* he directs his narrative toward that moment *after* which nothing can be changed, and he studies it with an intensity that magnifies and clarifies almost imperceptible changes in feeling and thought. As in Eliot's novels, so in the tales of this collection, there comes a moment requiring a decision that is irrevocable and that, once taken, sets irreversible consequences in motion. Crabbe's characters in these tales, like those in Eliot's novels, must choose, and must do so with faculties vitiated by old weaknesses and old defeats, overborne by sudden indulgences and by powerful pressures exerted by outside agents and external events. Both Eliot and Crabbe seek to delineate the most subtle of our self-defeats. In short, if Crabbe took much from the novel, it must be remembered that in the year George Eliot was born, he was working in the verse tale with the same moral and technical problems that she superbly mastered in her novels. The movement from Godwin and Inchbald and Edgeworth to Crabbe and then to Eliot and on to James is something of a full circle in the history of English fiction.

NOTES

1. I use the term *Augustan* in the same sense as that of F. R. Leavis in *Revaluation* (New York, 1947), p. 105, as a literary tradition to be distinguished from "the various Miltonic strains" of the eighteenth century, from what Josephine Miles has called "the sublime poem" in *Eras and Modes in English Poetry* (Berkeley and Los Angeles, Calif.,1957), pp. 48–77.

The weight of recent scholarship and critical opinion is that, though Crabbe brought new experience and attitudes to bear on his materials, his loyalty to Augustan satire underlies all his poetry. Oliver Sigworth's discussion is particularly helpful; he observes that Crabbe's realism and his "low" detail is derived from Augustan satire and that this surface likeness is a sign of Crabbe's deeper agreement with the Augustan satiric tradition (*Nature's Sternest Painter: Five Essays on the Poetry of George Crabbe* [Tucson, Ariz., 1965], pp. 17–21, *passim*). Leavis also identifies Crabbe as part of the Augustan tradition (*Revaluation,* pp. 124–29), and W. C. Brown has assessed Crabbe's relation to the heroic couplet in *The Triumph of Form* (Chapel Hill, N.C., 1948), p. 161–87. Karl Kroeber, in his study of romantic narrative art, sees Crabbe as an Augustan artist, untouched by organic art, except perhaps in *Tales of the Hall* (*Romantic Narrative Art* [Madison, Wis., 1960], pp. 115–21). On the other hand, W. E. Broman, in attempting to assess Crabbe's reputation in the early nineteenth century finds him "as much an integral part of the trends of the early nineteenth century as Scott or Byron" ("Factors in Crabbe's Eminence in the Early Nineteenth Century," *Modern Philology* 51 [1953]:42–49). Lilian Haddakin has observed that Crabbe was interested in representing a "process of the mind" in *The Poetry of Crabbe* (London, 1955), pp. 104–5, while Robert L. Chamberlain sees Crabbe as both an Augustan and romantic,.but his definition of romanticism includes a number of perfectly valid Augustan elements (*George Crabbe* [New York, 1965], pp. 104–11). Varley Lang has shown how Crabbe mastered the art of writing the satiric character, perhaps the chief vehicle of Augustan satire that was concerned above all with the minds and manners of men ("Crabbe and the Eighteenth Century," *ELH* 5 (1938):305–33); Arthur Sale has demonstrated that, in mastering this, Crabbe laid the foundation for his later narrative art ("The Development of Crabbe's Narrative Art," *Cambridge Journal* 5 (1952): 480–98); and John Speirs has placed Crabbe in the line of Pope and Johnson and pointed to his literary kinship with Austen ("Crabbe as Master of the Verse Tale," *Oxford Review* 2[1966]:3–40).

2. Rachel Trickett, *The Honest Muse: Study in Augustan Verse* (Oxford, 1967).

3. George Crabbe, "Memoirs of Eminent Persons: The Rev. Geo. Crabbe (by himself)," *New Monthly Magazine* 4(1816):512.

4. For Crabbe's early work, see "Juvenilia," in *Poems,* ed. A. W. Ward, 3 vols. (Cambridge, Eng., 1905–1907), 1:1–71—hereafter cited as *Poems.* For quotations from Crabbe's poetry, line numbers will be given in the text; pagination for the entire tale will be given in the first footnote reference to each tale.

5. For a discussion of midcentury satire, see Andrew M. Wilkinson, "The Decline of English Verse Satire in the Middle Years of the Eighteenth Century," *RES* n.s. 3(1952):222–33. See also H. D. Weinbrot, *The Formal Strain: Studies in Augustan Imitation and Satire* (Chicago, 1969). A particularly valuable discussion is W. B. Carnochan's "Satire, Sublimity, and Sentiment: Theory and Practice in Post-Augustan Satire." *PMLA* 85(1970):260–67.

6. George Crabbe, Jr., *The Life of George Crabbe by his Son,* in *The Poetical Works of the Rev. George Crabbe* (London, 1851) p. 37.

7. "In the course of the year 1799, he opened a communication with Mr. Hatchard . . . and was encouraged to prepare for publication a series of poems sufficient to fill a volume—among others, one on the Scripture story of Naaman; another, strange contrast! entitled 'Gipsy Will'; and a third founded on the legend of the Pedlar of Swaffham. But before . . . committing his reputation to the hazards of a new appearance, he judiciously paused to consult the well-known taste of the Reverend Richard Turner. . . . This friendly critic advised further revision, and his own mature opinion coinciding with that thus modestly hinted, he finally rejected the tales I have named altogether; deferred for a further period of eight years his reappearance as a poetical author . . ." (Crabbe, Jr., *Life,* p. 47).

8. See John W. Draper, "The Metrical Tale in XVIII-Century England," *PMLA* 52(1937):390–97.

9. A. M. Broadley and Walter Jerrold, *The Romance of an Elderly Poet* (London, 1913), p. 136.

10. Letter to Mary Leadbeater, Dec. 1, 1816, *The Leadbeater Papers,* ed. Mary Leadbeater (London, 1862), 2:340–41.

11. For a discussion of the eighteenth century's understanding of the term *mind,* see Paul K. Alkon, *Samuel Johnson and Moral Discipline* (Evanston, Ill., 1967), pp. 44–84.

NOTES TO CHAPTER 2

1. See Meyer Abrams, *The Mirror and the Lamp: Romantic Theory and the Critical Tradition* (New York, 1953).

2. "Schools," *Poems*, 1:523–24.

3. *The Art of Poetry Written in French by Sieur de Boileau . . . Made English by Sir William Soames, Since Revis'd by John Dryden, Esq.* (London, 1710), p. 16.

4. The best English discussion of the genre of satire remains Dryden's "A Discourse Concerning the Original and Progress of Satire," *Of Dramatic Poesy and Other Critical Essays*, ed. George Watson (London, 1964), 2:72–155.

5. John Brown, "An Essay on Satire, Occasioned by the Death of Mr. Pope," *The Works of the British Poets*, ed. Robert Anderson (London, 1795), 10:879.

6. Alexander Pope, "First Satire of the Second Book of Horace Imitated," *Poems: Imitations of Horace*, ed. John Butt (London and New Haven, 1961), 4:11.

7. For Boileau's reputation, see A. F. B. Clark, *Boileau and the French Classical Critics in England (1660–1830)* (Paris, 1925); for Pope's reputation in the early nineteenth century, see Upali Amarasinghe, *Dryden and Pope in the Early 19th Century* (Cambridge, 1962).

8. Paul Leedy, "Genres Criticism and the Significance of Warton's Essay on Pope," *Journal of English and German Philology* 45(1946):145.

9. Joseph Warton, *An Essay on the Genius and Writings of Pope*, 5th ed. (London, 1806), 2:402–3.

10. Ian Jack, *Augustan Satire* (London, 1952), p. 156.

11. William Lisle Bowles, *Letters to Lord Byron on a Question of Poetical Criticism*, 2d ed. (London, 1821), pp. 5–6.

12. Joseph Trapp, *Lectures on Poetry* (London, 1742), pp. 13–18, *passim*.

13. Thomas Twining, "On Poetry Considered as an Imitative Art," *Eighteenth Century Critical Essays*, ed. Scott Elledge (Ithaca, N. Y., 1961), 2:984–1004.

14. John Dennis, "The Advancement and Reformation of Modern Poetry," *Critical Works*, ed. Edward N. Hooker (Baltimore, Md., 1939), 1:215–16. See also Abrams, p. 75.

15. Sir William Jones, "On the Arts Commonly Called Imitative," *Eighteenth Century Critical Essays*, ed. Elledge, 2:872–81; see also Abrams, p. 87–88.

16. Hugh Blair, *Lectures on Poetry and Belles Lettres* (London, 1823), p. 511.

17. Richard Payne Knight, *An Analytical Inquiry into the Principles of Taste*, 2d. ed. (London, 1805), pp. 391–92.

18. W. R. Keast, "The Theoretical Foundations of Johnson's Criticism," *Critics and Criticism: Ancient and Modern*, ed. Ronald S. Crane (Chicago, 1952), p. 398.

19. "Examples are pictures, and strike the Senses, nay raise the Passions, and call in those (the strongest and most general of all motives) to the aid of reformation." Alexander Pope, *Correspondence*, ed. George Sherburn (Oxford, 1956), 3:419.

20. Dennis, *Critical Works*, 1:215.

21. This question was, of course, widely discussed during the eighteenth century; David Hume's "Of Tragedy" is probably the best-known discussion of the

subject *(Essays Moral, Political and Literary* [Oxford, 1963], pp. 221–30). For a criticism of the views summarized and offered by Hume, see George Campbell, *The Philosophy of Rhetoric,* ed. Lloyd F. Bitzer (Carbondale, Ill., 1963), pp. 112–38.

22. John Aikin and Anna L. Barbauld, "On the Objects of Terror," *Miscellaneous Pieces in Prose,* 3d ed. (London, 1792), pp. 119–20.

23. Payne Knight, *Analytical Inquiry,* p. 329.

24. Dugald Stewart, *Elements of the Philosophy of the Human Mind,* in *Collected Works,* ed. Sir William Hamilton (Edinburgh, 1854), 2:444.

25. "Preface to Lyrical Ballads, with Pastoral and Other Poems," *Literary Criticism of William Wordsworth,* ed. Paul M. Zall (Lincoln, Neb., 1966), p. 47.

26. From *The Letters of William and Dorothy Wordsworth: The Middle Years,* ed. Ernest de Selincourt, 1:244, quoted in Oliver Sigworth, *Nature's Sternest Painter: Five Essays on the Poetry of George Crabbe* (Tucson, Ariz., 1965), p. 62.

27. Samuel Taylor Coleridge, *The Table Talk and Omniana,* ed. T. Ashe (London, 1923), p. 276.

28. Frances Ann Kemble, *Records of a Girlhood,* 2d ed. (New York, 1883), p. 385.

29. "Preface," *Poems,* 1:96–97.

30. "Schools," *Poems,* 1:524.

31. "Preface," *Poems,* 2:11.

32. "Preface," *Poems,* 1:277.

33. Quoted in Amarasinghe, *Dryden and Pope,* p. 74.

34. A recent example is Robert L. Chamberlain, who fails to assess either the realities of Crabbe's situation or his defensiveness; see his *George Crabbe* (New York, 1965), pp. 103–4; see also Patricia Hodgart and Theodore Redpath, *Romantic Perspectives* (London, 1964), pp. 84–87.

35. Review of *The Borough, Monthly Review* 61 (1810):409; Francis Jeffrey, "Review of *The Borough,*" *Edinburgh Review,* 16 (1810):53.

36. Sigworth, *Nature's Sternest Painter,* pp. 43, 157.

37. William Hazlitt, *The Spirit of the Age,* in *Complete Works,* ed. P. P. Howe (London, 1932), 11:168.

38. Jeffrey, "Review of *The Borough,*" *Edinburgh Review* 16:38–39.

39. Jeffrey, "Review of *Tales in Verse,*" *Edinburgh Review* 20 (1812):277–78; "Review of *Poems,*" *Edinburgh Review* 12 (1808):148–51, *passim.*

40. Jeffrey, "Review of *The Borough,*" *Edinburgh Review* 16:53.

41. Jeffrey, "Review of *Tales in Verse,*" *Edinburgh Review* 20:278–79.

42. Jeffrey, "Review of *The Borough,*" *Edinburgh Review* 16:31.

43. Review of *The Borough, Monthly Review* 61:404.

44. [Robert Grant] "Review of *The Borough,*" *Quarterly Review* 4(1810):281.

45. Review of *The Borough, Christian Observer* 10(1811):504.

46. Review of *Tales of the Hall, Christian Observer* 18(1819):650–51.

47. A. M. Broadley and Walter Jerrold, *Romance of an Elderly Poet* (London, 1913), p. 242.

48. Trapp, *Lectures,* pp. 13–14.

49. Twining, in *Eighteenth Century Critical Essays,* ed. Elledge, 2:989–92.

50. Joseph Addison, "No. 408, Wed., June 18, 1712," *The Spectator,* ed. Donald F. Bond (Oxford, 1965), 3:526.

51. Samuel Johnson, "No. 49, Tues. 4 Sept. 1750," *The Rambler,* ed. W. J. Bate and Albrecht B. Strauss, The Yale Edition of the Works of Samuel Johnson (New Haven and London, 1969), 1:263–65, *passim.*

52. Thomas Reid, *Essays on the Powers of the Human Mind* (Edinburgh, 1819), 3:215.

53. Francis Hutcheson, *An Essay on the Nature and Conduct of the Passions and Affections with Illustrations on the Moral Sense,* 3d ed. with adds. (London, 1742), p. 29.

54. Reid, *Essays,* 3:218, 215–16.

55. Lord Kames [Henry Home], *Elements of Criticism* (Edinburgh, 1762), 2:131–40.

56. Brewster Rogerson, "The Art of Painting the Passions," *Journal of the History of Ideas* 14 (1953):88–89.

57. Baron Paul Heinrich Dietrich von Holbach, *The System of Nature: or, The Laws of the Moral and Physical World* (London, 1884), p. 90.

58. William Godwin, *Enquiry Concerning Political Justice and Its Influence on Morals and Happiness,* ed. F. E. I. Priestley, facs. of the 3d ed. corr. (Toronto, 1946), 1:425–26.

59. Hugh Blair, "On the Slavery of Vice," *Sermons* (London, 1794), 4:206.

60. Blair, "On the Government of the Heart [Part II]," *Sermons* (London, 1780), 2:66–67.

61. Blair, "On the Slavery of Vice," *Sermons,* 4:207–10, *passim.*

62. Holbach, *System of Nature,* p. 90.

NOTES TO CHAPTER 3

1. Hugh Blair, *Lectures on Poetry and Belles Lettres* (London, 1823), p. 584.

2. Anna Seward, *Letters* (Edinburgh, 1811), 1:236.

3. Quoted from a "Review of Gregory's *Letters on Literature, Taste, and Composition,*" *Monthly Review* 61(1810):249.

4. Josephine Miles, *Eras and Modes in English Poetry* (Berkeley and Los Angeles, 1957), p. 50.

5. Alexander Pope, *Correspondence,* ed. George Sherburn (Oxford, 1956), 2:202–3.

6. Lord Kames [Henry Home], *Elements of Criticism* (Edinburgh, 1762), 3:174–76.

7. Joseph Trapp, *Lectures on Poetry* (London, 1742), pp. 131–32.

8. Robert Dodsley, *An Essay on Fable,* The Augustan Reprint Society no. 112 (Los Angeles, Calif., 1965), p. lxxvi.

9. Thomas Parnell, "Essay on the Different Styles of Poetry," *The Works of the*

English Poets, ed. Alexander Chalmers (London, 1810), 9:413, 415 (hereafter cited as *English Poets*).

10. John Newbery, *The Art of Poetry on a New Plan* (London, 1762), 1:235. For a survey of the eighteenth-century verse tale with a system of classification different from mine, see John W. Draper, "The Metrical Tale in XVIII-Century England," *PMLA* 52(1937):390–97.

The authorship of *Poetry on a New Plan* is uncertain; "Newbery" is used throughout this study merely as a term of convenience.

11. Robert Dodsley, for one, classified as *fable* all compositions—epic, dramatic, Aesopean—whose purpose is to "illustrate some one moral or prudential maxim." It is to this end, he said, that "the composition in all its parts must be directed," the action serving "to enforce the maxim." Under the term *tale* Dodsley classifies those narratives, whether serious or comic, that "imply no sort of Moral" and that are not "contrived on purpose to teach and to imprint some Truth" that is clearly illustrated "in the very catastrophe" (*Essay,* pp. lvii–lix, *passim*). However, as Dodsley admitted, the fable was by definition allegorical, with mice and lions, mountains and molehills representing the passions, virtues, and vices of human beings·(*Essay,* pp. lxviii–lxxii). A narrative whose characters were human beings is not properly a fable, so the short, instructive, allegorical narrative whose agents were nonhuman was called a fable, while the narrative whose characters were human beings was a tale, whether instructive or not (Samuel Johnson, "John Gay," *Lives of the English Poets,* ed. Birkbeck Hill (Oxford, 1905), 2:283.

12. Thomas Parnell, "The Hermit," *English Poets,* 9:367; William Whitehead, "The Dog. A Tale," *English Poets,* 17:217; Robert Burns, "Tam O' Shanter," *Poems and Songs,* ed. James Kingsley (Oxford, 1968), 2:564; Hannah More, "The Plum-Cakes: Or, the Farmer and his Three Sons," *Works* (London, 1854) 5:380. It is not surprising that pentameter preceptive tales are usually more "serious" than tetrameter tales. Only a few pentameter preceptive tales were written, whereas the tetrameter version was very popular. The last pentameter preceptive tale that I have been able to find is Walter Harte's "Eulogius: or, the Charitable Mason," published in 1743. The "low" tetrameter tale flourished from the beginning to the end of the eighteenth century; Prior and Swift were among its leading practitioners, and "Tam O' Shanter," published in 1791, was among the last of its kind.

13. Oliver Goldsmith, *Miscellaneous Works* (London, 1801), 1:29.

14. John Gay, "A True Story of an Apparition," *English Poets,* 10:506–7.

15. Joseph Warton, *An Essay on the Genius and Writings of Pope,* 5th ed. (London, 1806), 2:160.

16. Sir Walter Scott, "Ann Radcliffe," *On Novelists and Fiction,* ed. Ioan Williams (London, 1968), p. 110.

17. "The Lover's Journey," *Poems,* 2:135–44.

18. Tales ending with a precept are "The Patron," "The Widow's Tale," "Arabella," " 'Squire Thomas," "The Struggles of Conscience," "The Wager," "The Convert," "The Learned Boy." Tales beginning with a precept or thesis are

"The Dumb Orators," "Edward Shore," " Procrastination," "The Lover's Journey," "The Parting Hour," "Resentment." Tales with neither a preceptive beginning nor conclusion are "The Gentleman Farmer," "The Frank Courtship," "The Mother," "Jesse and Colin," "The 'Squire and the Priest," "The Confidant," and "The Brothers." In *Tales of the Hall* Crabbe, rather surprisingly, employs precept more frequently than in *Tales in Verse*.

19. Karl Kroeber, *Romantic Narrative Art* (Madison, Wis., 1960), pp. 118–19.

20. Oliver Sigworth, *Nature's Sternest Painter; Five Essays on the Poetry of George Crabbe* (Tucson, Ariz., 1965), pp. 116–18.

21. Jonathan Swift, *Poems,* ed. Harold Williams, 2nd ed. (Oxford, 1958), 1:221–25.

22. "William Bailey," *Poems,* 3:127–46.

23. William Whitehead, "Variety. A Tale for Married People," *English Poets,* 17:234–37.

24. " 'Squire Thomas," *Poems,* 2:160–69.

NOTES TO CHAPTER 4

1. Lord Kames [Henry Home], *Elements of Criticism* (Edinburgh, 1762), 3:221–22.

2. For a discussion of the complications attending pity as pleasure, see George Campbell, "Of the cause of that pleasure which we receive from objects or representations that excite pity and other painful feelings," *The Philosophy of Rhetoric,* ed. Lloyd F. Bitzer (Carbondale, Ill., 1963), pp. 112–38; see also John Hawkesworth, "No. 110, Sat., Nov. 24, 1753," *The Adventurer,* in *The British Essayists,* ed. Robert Lynam (London, 1827), 15:186–90, and Samuel Johnson, "No. 60, Sat., Oct. 13, 1750," *The Rambler,* ed. W. J. Bate and Albrecht B. Strauss, The Yale Edition of the Works of Samuel Johnson (New Haven and London, 1969), 3:318–19.

3. Hugh Blair, "On the Government of the Heart" [Part II] *Sermons* (London, 1780), 2:55.

4. See Brewster Rogerson, "The Art of Painting the Passions," *Journal of the History of Ideas* 14(1953):70, for the pleasure eighteenth-century audiences derived from the display of the passions.

5. See Thomas Percy, *Reliques of Ancient English Poetry* (Edinburgh, 1858), 2:21; William Shenstone, *Letters,* ed. Marjorie Williams (Oxford, 1939), p. 178,n.1; Matthew Prior, *Literary Works,* ed. H. Bunker Wright and Monroe K. Spears (Oxford, 1959), 2:909–10.

6. Alexander Pope, *Correspondence,* ed. George Sherburn (Oxford, 1956), 2:369–70.

7. William Shenstone's "Love and Honour," Edward Young's "The Force of Religion; Or, Vanquish'd Love," and James Montgomery's "The Wanderer of Switzerland" are pathetic tales; owing to limitations of space, I have not discussed these poems.

8. "The Not-Browne Mayd," Percy, *Reliques,* 2:21–35.

9. Matthew Prior, "Henry and Emma, A Poem Upon the Model of the Nut-browne Maid. To Chloe," *Literary Works,* 1:278–300. For a discussion of this poem, see Karl Kroeber, *Romantic Narrative Art* (Madison, Wis., 1960), pp. 13–19.

10. Lady Mary Wortley Montagu, *Complete Letters,* ed. Robert Halsband (Oxford, 1967), 3:68.

11. Samuel Johnson, "Matthew Prior," *Lives of the English Poets,* ed. Birkbeck Hill (Oxford, 1905), 2:201, 203.

12. Prior, "To a Young Gentleman in Love. A Tale," *Literary Works,* 1:193–95. Johnson says that this poem "has hardly a just claim to the title of a 'Tale'" (*Lives,* 2:201).

13. "The Natural Death of Love," *Poems,* 3:49–60.

14. Oliver Goldsmith, "Edwin and Angelina," *Collected Works,* ed. Arthur Friedman (Oxford, 1966), 4:199–206.

15. Edmund Cartwright, "Armine and Elvira. A Legendary Tale," *The English Anthology,* ed. Joseph Ritson (London, 1794), 3:272–95.

16. John Newbery, *The Art of Poetry on a New Plan* (London, 1762), 1:149.

17. Oliver Goldsmith, *Miscellaneous Works* (London, 1801), 2:13.

18. James Thomson, "Palemon and Lavinia," *The Seasons: Autumn,* in *Poetical Works,* ed. J. Logie Robertson (London, 1908), pp. 139–44.

19. William Richardson, "Rowena," *Poems, Chiefly Rural,* 4th ed. (Glasgow, 1781), pp. 123–25.

20. "Sir Eustace Grey," *Poems,* 1:238–51.

21. "The Hall of Justice," *Poems,* 1:252–60.

22. Anna Seward, "Preface," *Louisa: A Poetical Novel* (Lichfield, 1784) [pp. i–ii].

23. Thomas Parnell, "The Hermit," *English Poets,* 9:367.

24. Seward, *Letters* (Edinburgh, 1811), 1:357–58.

25. "The Mother," *Poems,* 2:114–23.

26. Robert Bloomfield, "Preface," *Rural Tales, Ballads, and Songs* (London, 1802), pp. iii–iv.

27. Francis Jeffrey also complained of the lack of focus and coherent structure in *Marmion* ("Review of *Marmion* . . . ," *Edinburgh Review* 12 [1808]: 2).

28. "Jesse and Colin," *Poems,* 2:171–84.

29. Maria Edgeworth, "The Contrast," *Tales and Novels* (London, 1893), 2:343–45, *passim.*

30. Josephine Miles, *Eras and Modes in English Poetry* (Berkeley and Los Angeles, Calif., 1957), p. 49.

31. George Kubler, *The Shape of Time* (New Haven and London, 1971), p. 47.

NOTES TO CHAPTER 5

1. See Francis Jeffrey, "Review of *Tales in Verse,*" *Edinburgh Review* 20 (1812): 278–79; Alfred Ainger, *Crabbe* (New York, 1903), p. 104; F. R. Leavis, *Revaluation*

(New York, 1947), p. 125; Oliver Sigworth, *Nature's Sternest Painter: Five Essays on the Poetry of George Crabbe* (Tucson, Ariz., 1965), p. 127; Karl Kroeber, *Romantic Narrative Art* (Madison, Wis., 1960), p. 120; John Speirs, "Crabbe as Master of the Verse Tale," *Oxford Review* 1(1966):3–40.

2. George Crabbe, Jr., *The Life of George Crabbe by his Son,* in *The Poetical Works of the Rev. George Crabbe* (London, 1851), p. 44.

3. Hugh Blair, *Lectures on Poetry and Belles Lettres* (London, 1823), pp. 546, 509.

4. Samuel Richardson, "Preface," *Clarissa Harlowe,* in *Works,* ed. Sir Leslie Stephen (London, 1883), 4:xiii.

5. Elizabeth Inchbald, "Novel-writing," *The Artist; A Collection of Essays,* ed. Prince Hoare (London, 1810), 1:xiv, 14–15.

6. [William Hazlitt] *"The Wanderer: or, Female Difficulties, A Novel,* by Madame D'Arblay," *Edinburgh Review* 24(1815):320.

7. Quoted from [Richard Whately], *"Northanger Abbey* and *Persuasion,"* Quarterly Review 24(1821):352 [originally appeared in Scott's review of *Emma, Quarterly Review* 14(1815):188–201.]

8. [Whately] 24:353, 357.

9. Crabbe, Jr., *Life,* pp. 46–47.

10. Inchbald submitted *Nature and Art* "to her three literary friends, Mr. Holcroft, Mr. Godwin, and Mr. Hardinge . . ."(James Boaden, *Memoirs of Mrs. Inchbald* [London, 1833], 1:315). A few years later Maria Edgeworth submitted her work to Inchbald for criticism; the correspondence ensuing offers revealing commentary on their art of fiction *(Ibid.,* 2:129–212, *passim).* Amelia Opie and Mary Leadbeater, both friends of Crabbe, are linked with this group. Opie inherited the pathetic side of Inchbald's art; Edgeworth adapted Inchbald's preceptive vein to the Edgeworthian system. In addition, Mary Wollstonecraft's *Original Stories* (1788) and Hannah More's *Repository Tracts* (1795) are prototypes of Edgeworth's work.

11. Thomas Holcroft, *The Adventures of Hugh Trevor* (London, 1794), 1:vi–vii.

12. For example, Holcroft has a lengthy episode about the sufferings of a boy apprenticed to a sadistic master, in many ways like "Peter Grimes"; the miseries of the young poet in Crabbe's "The Patron" have much in common with those described by Holcroft in his account of patronage.

13. William Godwin, "Preface," *The Adventures of Caleb Williams, or, Things as They Are,* ed. George Sherburn (New York and Toronto, 1960), p. xxiii— hereafter cited as *Caleb Williams).*

14. "Godwin's own Account of *Caleb Williams," Caleb Williams,* p. xxviii.

15. "The Parting Hour," *Poems,* 2:28–40.

16. Review of *Tales of the Hall, Christian Observer* (1819): 657.

17. J. M. S. Tompkins, *The Popular Novel in England 1770–1800* (Lincoln, Neb., 1961), pp. 309–11.

18. Anna L. Barbauld, "On the Origin and Progress of Novel-Writing," *The British Novelists* (London, 1810), 1:55–57, *passim* (hereafter cited as *British Novelists).*

19. "Ellen Orford," *Poems,* 1:470–79.

20. "Resentment," *Poems,* 2:229–41.

21. "The Mother," *Poems,* 2:114–23.

22. Crabbe, Jr., *Life,* p. 44.

23. Elizabeth Inchbald, *Nature and Art,* in *British Novelists,* 27:375.

24. Barbauld, *British Novelists,* 28:iv.

25. Boaden, *Memoirs* 2:152–54, *passim.* Mary Leadbeater, an imitator of Edgeworth, writes to Crabbe: "The characters . . . have the convincing power of reality over the mind, and *I* maintain that the pictures are drawn from life. To enquire whether this is the case is the excuse which I make to myself for writing this letter" (Mary Leadbeater, ed., *The Leadbeater Papers,* 2d ed. [London, 1862], 2:336–37). Crabbe replied that nearly all his characters were drawn from life (*Leadbeater Papers,* 2:340–41).

26. Maria Edgeworth, "Preface to the Third Edition," *Patronage,* 3d ed. (London, 1815), 1:v–vi.

27. R. L. Edgeworth, " 'Preface' to *Moral Tales,*" *Tales and Novels of Maria Edgeworth* (London, 1893), 1:vi.

28. R. L. Edgeworth, Letter to Elizabeth Inchbald, Oct. 2, 1809, Boaden, *Memoirs,* 2:150.

29. Maria Edgeworth, Letter to Elizabeth Inchbald, Feb. 14, 1814, *ibid.,* 2:194–95.

30. *Leadbeater Papers,* 2:370–71.

31. "The Learned Boy," *Poems,* 2:277–91.

32. Maria Edgeworth, "Rosana," *Tales and Novels* 2:194–244.

33. "The Brothers," *Poems,* 2:265–75.

34. Review of *Tales of the Hall, Christian Observer* 18(1819):659–61.

NOTES TO CHAPTER 6

1. George Crabbe, "The Description of the Wicked," *Posthumous Sermons,* ed. John D. Hastings (London, 1850), pp. 56–65 *passim* (hereafter cited as *Post. Sermons*).

2. Lilian Haddakin, *The Poetry of George Crabbe* (London, 1955), pp. 88–89.

3. Alexander Pope, "Epistle III. To Allen Lord Bathurst," *Poems: Epistles to Several Persons,* ed. F. W. Bateson (London and New Haven, 1961), 3:ii, 121–25 (l. 339–402).

4. Varley H. Lang, "Crabbe and the Eighteenth Century," *ELH* 5(1938):315.

5. "The Parish-Clerk," *Poems,* 1:461–68.

6. Sir Walter Scott, *Poetical Works,* ed. J. Logie Robertson (London, 1904), p. 109.

7. "Preface," *Poems,* 1:278–79.

8. "Peter Grimes," *Poems,* 1:492–501.

9. "Procrastination," *Poems,* 2:57–66.

10. Lord Kames [Henry Home], *Elements of Criticism* (Edinburgh, 1762), 3:377.

11. "The Convert," *Poems*, 2:252–63.

12. "The Patron," *Poems*, 2:68–86.

13. "Edward Shore," *Poems*, 2:146–58.

14. "The Struggles of Conscience," *Poems*, 2:186–98.

15. "The Gentleman Farmer," *Poems*, 2:42–55.

16. "Arabella," *Poems*, 2:125–33.

17. "The Wager," *Poems*, 2:243–50.

18. "The Parting Hour," *Poems*, 2:28–40.

19. "Resentment," *Poems*, 2:229–41.

20. "The Hall," *Poems*, 2:306.

21. "Schools," *Poems*, 1:524.

22. See René Huchon, *George Crabbe and his Times 1754–1832* (New York, 1907), pp. 386–88, and A. M. Broadley and Walter Jerrold, *The Romance of an Elderly Poet* (London, 1913).

23. "Delay Has Danger," *Poems*, 3:27–47.

24. "The Maid's Story," *Poems*, 2:452–79.

25. "Lady Barbara; or, The Ghost," *Poems*, 3:75–99.

26. Warren Derry, *Dr. Parr: A Portrait of the Whig Dr. Johnson* (Oxford, 1966), pp. 198–205.

27. "Gretna Green," *Poems*, 3:62–73.

SELECTIVE BIBLIOGRAPHY

WORKS BY CRABBE

Crabbe, George. "Memoirs of Eminent Persons: the Rev. Geo. Crabbe (by himself)." *New Monthly Magazine* 4(1816):511–17.

————. *New Poems by George Crabbe.* Edited by Arthur Pollard. Liverpool: Liverpool University Press, 1960.

————. *Poems.* Edited by A. W. Ward. 3 vols. Cambridge: University Press, 1905–1907.

————. *Posthumous Sermons.* Edited by John D. Hastings. London, 1850.

WORKS RELATING TO CRABBE

Ainger, Alfred C. *Crabbe.* London: Macmillan & Co., 1903.

Bareham, T. "Crabbe's Studies of Derangement and Hallucination." *Orbis Litterarum* 24(1969):161–81.

Batdorf, Franklin Pierce. "A Study of George Crabbe's Tales." *Cornell University Abstracts of Theses . . . for the Doctor's Degree, 1942.* Ithaca, N. Y.: Cornell University Press, 1943.

Bowers, Clementian. *Characterization in the Narrative Poetry of*

George Crabbe. Abstract of a Dissertation. Washington, D.C.: Catholic University of America Press, 1959.

Broadley, A. M., and Jerrold, Walter. *The Romance of an Elderly Poet. A Hitherto Unknown Chapter in the Life of George Crabbe.* . . . London: Stanley Paul & Co., 1913.

Broman, W. E. "Factors in Crabbe's Eminence in the Early Nineteenth Century." *Modern Philology* 51(1953):42–49.

Brown, Wallace Cable. *The Triumph of Form: A Study of the Later Masters of the Heroic Couplet.* Chapel Hill: University of North Carolina Press, 1948.

Carnochan, W. B. "Satire, Sublimity, and Sentiment: Theory and Practice in Post-Augustan Satire." *PMLA* 85(1970):260–67.

Chamberlain, Robert L. *George Crabbe.* Twayne's English Authors. New York: Twayne, 1965.

Crabbe, George, Jr. *The Life of George Crabbe by his Son.* In *The Poetical Works of the Rev. George Crabbe.* London, 1851.

Cruttwell, Patrick. "The Last Augustan." *Hudson Review* 7(1955):533–54.

Duncan-Jones, E. E. "Jane Austen and Crabbe." *RES*, n.s. 5(1954): 174.

Evans, John H. *The Poems of George Crabbe: A Literary and Historical Study.* London: Sheldon Press, 1933.

Haddakin, Lilian. *The Poetry of Crabbe.* London: Chatto & Windus, 1955.

Hodgart, Patricia, and Redpath, Theodore. *Romantic Perspectives. The Work of Crabbe, Blake, Wordsworth, and Coleridge as Seen by their Contemporaries.* London: George Harrap & Co., 1964.

Huchon, René. *George Crabbe and his Times 1754–1832: A Critical and Biographical Study.* Translated from the French by Frederick Clarke. London: John Murray, 1907.

Kebbel, Thomas E. *Life of George Crabbe.* London, 1888.

Lang, Varley. "Crabbe and the Eighteenth Century." *ELH* 5(1938):305–33.

Leadbeater, Mary. *The Leadbeater Papers. The Annals of Ballitore.* . . . 2 vols. London and Dublin, 1862.

Leavis, F. R. *Revaluation.* New York: G. W. Stewart, 1947.

Pollard, Arthur. "George Crabbe's Theology." *Church Quarterly Review* 157(1956):309–16.

Sale, Arthur. "The Development of Crabbe's Narrative Art." *Cambridge Journal* 5(1952):480–98.

Sigworth, Oliver. *Nature's Sternest Painter: Five Essays on the Poetry of George Crabbe.* Tucson: University of Arizona Press, 1965.

Speirs, John. "Crabbe as Master of the Verse Tale." *Oxford Review* 2(1966):3–40.

Spingarn, Lawrence P. "George Crabbe as Realist." *University of Kansas City Review* 17(1950):60–65.

Thomas, W. K. "Crabbe's Workhouse." *Huntington Library Quarterly* 32(1969):149–61.

―――. "George Crabbe: Not Quite the Sternest." *Studies in Romanticism* 7(1968):166–75.

CONTEMPORARY REVIEWS OF CRABBE'S WORK*

[Grant, Robert.] Review of *The Borough. Quarterly Review* 4(1810):281–312.

[Jeffrey, Francis.] Review of *The Borough. Edinburgh Review* 16(1810):30–55.

―――. Review of *Poems. Edinburgh Review* 12(1808):131–51.

―――. Review of *Tales in Verse. Edinburgh Review* 20(1812):277–305.

Review of *The Borough. Christian Observer* 10(1811):502–11.

Review of *Tales of the Hall. Christian Observer* 18(1819):650–68.

Review of *The Borough. Monthly Review* 61(1810):396–409.

POETRY

Anderson, Robert, ed. *The Works of the British Poets.* 14 vols. London, 1792–1795.

*Only reviews cited in the text are included. For other reviews of Crabbe, see Arthur Pollard, *Crabbe: The Critical Heritage* (London and Boston: Routledge & Kegan Paul, 1972).

Blake, William. *The Poetical Works of William Blake.* Edited by John Sampson. Oxford: Clarendon Press, 1947.

Bloomfield, Robert. *Rural Tales, Ballads, and Songs.* London, 1802.

Burns, Robert. *The Poems and Songs of Robert Burns.* Edited by James Kingsley. 3 vols. Oxford: Clarendon Press, 1968.

Byrom, John. "Poems." In *The Works of the English Poets.* Edited by Alexander Chalmers, vol. 15. London, 1810.

Cawthorn, James. "Poems." In *The Works of the English Poets.* Edited by Alexander Chalmers, vol. 14. London, 1810.

Chalmers, Alexander, ed. *The Works of the English Poets.* 21 vols. London, 1810.

Chatterton, Thomas. *The Complete Works of Thomas Chatterton: A Bicentenary Edition.* Edited by Donald S. Taylor in association with Benjamin B. Hoover. Oxford: Clarendon Press, 1971.

Churchill, Charles. *The Poetical Works of Charles Churchill.* Edited by Douglas Grant. Oxford: Clarendon Press, 1956.

Congreve, William. "Poems." In *The Works of the English Poets.* Edited by Alexander Chalmers, vol. 10. London, 1810.

Cowper, William. *Poetical Works.* Edited by H. S. Milford, 4th ed., with corrections and additions by Norma Russell. London: Oxford University Press, 1967.

Cunningham, John. "Poems." In *The Works of the English Poets.* Edited by Alexander Chalmers, vol. 14. London, 1810.

Dodsley, Robert. "Poems." In *The Works of the English Poets.* Edited by Alexander Chalmers, vol. 15. London, 1810.

————, ed. *A Collection of Poems by Several Hands.* 6 vols. London, 1765.

Dryden, John. *The Poems of John Dryden.* Edited by John Sargeaunt. London: Oxford University Press, 1948.

Duck, Stephen. *Alrick and Isabel, or the Unhappy Marriage: A Poem.* London, 1740.

Ellis, George. *Poetical Tales by Sir Gregory Gander.* Bath, 1778.

Gay, John. "Poems." In *The Works of the English Poets.* Edited by Alexander Chalmers, vol. 10. London, 1810.

Goldsmith, Oliver. *Collected Works of Oliver Goldsmith.* Edited by Arthur Friedman. 5 vols. Oxford: Clarendon Press, 1966.

Gray, Thomas. *The Complete Poems of Thomas Gray.* Edited by H. W. Starr and J. R. Hendrickson. Oxford: Clarendon Press, 1966.

Harte, Walter. "Poems." In *The Works of the English Poets.* Edited by Alexander Chalmers, vol. 16. London, 1810.

Hull, Thomas. *Moral Tales in Verse, Founded on Real Events.* 2 vols. London, 1797.

Jenyns, Soames. "Poems." In *The Works of the English Poets.* Edited by Alexander Chalmers, vol. 17. London, 1810.

King, William. "Poems." In *The Works of the English Poets.* Edited by Alexander Chalmers, vol. 9. London, 1810.

Lloyd, Charles. "Poems." In *The Works of the English Poets.* Edited by Alexander Chalmers, vol. 15. London, 1810.

Lovibond, Edward. "Poems." In *The Works of the English Poets.* Edited by Alexander Chalmers, vol. 16. London, 1810.

Mallet, David. "Poems." In *The Works of the English Poets.* Edited by Alexander Chalmers, vol. 14. London, 1810.

Montgomery, James. *The Wanderer of Switzerland, and Other Poems.* 3d. ed. London, 1806.

Moore, Edward. "Poems." In *The Works of the English Poets.* Edited by Alexander Chalmers, vol. 14. London, 1810.

More, Hannah. "Poems." In *Works,* vol. 5. London, 1853.

Parnell, Thomas. "Poems." In *The Works of the English Poets.* Edited by Alexander Chalmers, vol. 9. London, 1810.

Percy, Thomas. *The Hermit of Warkworth, A Northumbrian Ballad: In Three Fits.* London, 1771.

————. *Reliques of Ancient English Poetry.* Edited by Charles Cowden Clarke and with a memoir and critical introduction . . . by G. Gilfillan. 3 vols. Edinburgh, 1858.

Pope, Alexander. *The Twickenham Edition of the Poems of Alexander Pope.* John Butt, general editor. 10 vols. London: Methuen & Co.; New Haven: Yale University Press, 1961–1967.

Prior, Matthew. *The Literary Works of Matthew Prior.* Edited by H. Bunker Wright and Monroe K. Spears. 2 vols. Oxford: Clarendon Press, 1959.

Richardson, William. *Poems, Chiefly Rural.* 4th ed. Glasgow, 1781.

Ritson, Joseph, ed. *The English Anthology.* 3 vols. London, 1793–1794.

Scott, Sir Walter. *Poetical Works.* Edited by J. Logie Robertson. London: Henry Frowde, 1904.

Seward, Anna. *Louisa: A Poetical Novel, In Four Epistles.* Lichfield, 1784.

Shenstone, William. "Poems." In *The Works of the English Poets.* Edited by Alexander Chalmers, vol. 13. London, 1810.

Somerville, William. "Poems." In *The Works of the English Poets.* Edited by Alexander Chalmers, vol. 11. London, 1810.

[Stevenson, John Hall.] *Crazy Tales.* [n.p.] 1772.

Swift, Jonathan. *Poems.* Edited by Harold Williams. 3 vols. 2d. ed. Oxford: Clarendon Press, 1958.

Thomson, James. *Complete Poetical Works of James Thomson.* Edited by J. Logie Robertson. London: Henry Frowde, 1908.

Whitehead, William. "Poems." In *The Works of the English Poets.* Edited by Alexander Chalmers, vol. 17. London, 1810.

Williams, Helen Maria. *Edwin and Eltruda. A Legendary Tale.*

————. *Peru: A Poem.* London, 1784.

Young, Edward. "Poems." In *The Works of the English Poets.* Edited by Alexander Chalmers, vol. 13. London, 1810.

PROSE FICTION

Bage, Robert. *Man as He Is.* 4 vols. London, 1792.

————. *Man as He Is Not; or, Hermsprong.* vol. 48. *The British Novelists.* Edited by Anna L. Barbauld. London, 1810.

Barbauld, Anna L., ed. *The British Novelists.* 50 vols. London, 1810.

Edgeworth, Maria. *Patronage.* 4 vols. 3d ed. London, 1815.

————. *Tales and Novels.* 10 vols. London, 1893.

Godwin, William. *The Adventures of Caleb Williams, or, Things as They Are.* Edited by George Sherburn. New York and Toronto: Rinehart & Co., 1960.

————. *Fleetwood, or, the New Man of Feeling.* 3 vols. London, 1805.

————. *St. Leon; A Tale of the Sixteenth Century.* 4 vols. London, 1799.

Holcroft, Thomas. *The Adventures of Hugh Trevor.* 6 vols. London, 1794–1797.

————. *Anna St. Ives.* 7 vols. London, 1792.

Inchbald, Elizabeth. *Nature and Art.* In *The British Novelists.* Edited by Anna L. Barbauld, vol. 27. London, 1810.

————. *A Simple Story.* Edited by J. M. S. Tompkins. London: Oxford University Press, 1967.

Leadbeater, Mary. *Cottage Dialogues among the Irish Peasantry.* London, 1811.

Lee, Harriet, and Lee, Sophia. *Canterbury Tales.* 5 vols. London, 1797–1801.

More, Hannah. "Tales for the Common People." In vol. 1, pp. 249–86; vol. 2, pp. 5–236. *Works.* London, 1853.

Opie, Amelia. *The Father and Daughter, A Tale in Prose.* 2d ed. London, 1801.

Radcliffe, Ann. *The Mysteries of Udolpho.* vols. 45–47. *The British Novelists.* Edited by Anna L. Barbauld. London, 1810.

————. *The Romance of the Forest.* vols. 43–44. *The British Novelists.* Edited by Anna L. Barbauld. London, 1810.

Wollstonecraft, Mary. *Original Stories from Real Life; with Conversations Calculated to Regulate the Affections.* London, 1791.

THEORETICAL AND CRITICAL BACKGROUND:
PRIMARY SOURCES

Addison, Joseph, and Steele, Sir Richard. *The Spectator.* Edited by Donald F. Bond. 5 vols. Oxford: Clarendon Press, 1965.

Aikin, John, and Barbauld, Anna L. *Miscellaneous Pieces in Prose.* 3d ed. London, 1792.

Blair, Hugh. *Lectures on Poetry and Belles Lettres.* London, 1823.

————. *Sermons.* 5 vols. London, 1777–1801.

Boaden, James. *Memoirs of Mrs. Inchbald: Including her Familiar Correspondence.* . . . 2 vols. London, 1833.

Boileau-Despréaux, Nicolas. *The Art of Poetry Written in French by Sieur de Boileau* . . . *Made English by Sir William Soames, Since Revis'd by John Dryden, Esq.* London, 1710.

Bowles, William Lisle. *Letters to Lord Byron on a Question of Poetical Criticism.* 2d ed. London, 1821.

Campbell, George. *The Philosophy of Rhetoric.* . . . Edited by Lloyd F. Bitzer. Carbondale, Ill.: Southern Illinois University Press, 1963.

Coleridge, Samuel Taylor. *The Table Talk and Omniana.* Edited by T. Ashe. London: Bohn's Popular Library, 1923.

Dennis, John. *The Critical Works of John Dennis.* Edited by Edward Niles Hooker. 2 vols. Baltimore: The Johns Hopkins University Press, 1939–1943.

Dodsley, Robert. *An Essay on Fable.* Introduction by Jeanne K. Welcher and Richard Dircks. The Augustan Reprint Society No. 112. Los Angeles: William Andrews Clark Memorial Library, University of California, 1965.

Dryden, John. *Of Dramatic Poesy, and Other Critical Essays.* Edited by George Watson. 2 vols. London: J. M. Dent & Sons; New York: E. P. Dutton & Co., 1964.

Godwin, William. *Enquiry Concerning Political Justice and Its Influence on Morals and Happiness.* Edited by F. E. I. Priestley. 3 vols. Photographic facsimile of the 3d ed. corrected. Toronto: University of Toronto Press, 1946.

(Review of) Gregory's *Letters on Literature, Taste and Composition. Monthly Review* 61(1810):246–59.

Hawkesworth, John. "No. 110, Sat., Nov. 24, 1753." In *The Adventurer,* 15:186–90. *The British Essayists.* Edited by Robert Lynam. London, 1827.

Hayley, William. *An Essay on Epic Poetry; In Five Epistles to the Revd. Mr. Mason.* London, 1782.

[Hazlitt, William.] Review of *The Wanderer: or, Female Difficulties. A Novel. Edinburgh Review* 24(1815):320–38.

———. *The Spirit of the Age.* vol. 11. *Complete Works.* Edited by P.P. Howe. London and Toronto: J. M. Dent & Sons, 1932.

von Holbach, Baron Paul Heinrich Dietrich. *The System of Nature; or, The Laws of the Moral and Physical World.* London, 1884.

Hume, David. *Essays Moral, Political and Literary.* London: Oxford University Press, 1963.

Hutcheson, Francis. *An Essay on the Nature and Conduct of the Passions and Affections with Illustrations on the Moral Sense.* 3d ed. with additions. London, 1742.

Inchbald, Elizabeth. "Novel-Writing." In *The Artist; A Collection of Essays.* Edited by Prince Hoare, 1:14–15. London, 1810.

[Jeffrey, Francis.] Review of *Marmion. Edinburgh Review* 12(1808):1–35.

Johnson, Samuel. *Lives of the English Poets.* Edited by Birkbeck Hill. 3 vols. Oxford: Clarendon Press, 1905.

———. *The Rambler.* Edited by W. J. Bate and Albrecht B. Strauss, vols. 3, 4, 5 of The Yale Edition of the Works of Samuel Johnson. New Haven and London: Yale University Press, 1969.

Jones, Sir William. "On the Arts Commonly Called Imitative." In *Eighteenth-Century Critical Essays.* Edited by Scott Elledge, vol. 2. Ithaca, N. Y.: Cornell University Press, 1961.

Kames, Lord [Henry Home]. *Elements of Criticism.* 3 vols. Edinburgh, 1762.

Kemble, Frances Ann. *Records of a Girlhood.* 2d ed. New York, 1883.

Knight, Richard Payne. *An Analytical Inquiry into the Principles of Taste.* 2d ed. London, 1805.

Montagu, Lady Mary Wortley. *The Complete Letters of Lady Mary Wortley Montagu.* Edited by Robert Halsband. 3 vols. Oxford: Clarendon Press, 1965–1967.

Newbery, John [?]. *The Art of Poetry on a New Plan.* 2 vols. London, 1762.

Pope, Alexander. *The Correspondence of Alexander Pope.* Edited by George Sherburn. 5 vols. Oxford: Clarendon Press, 1956.

Reid, Thomas. *Essays on the Powers of the Human Mind. . . .* 3 vols. Edinburgh, 1819.

Scott, Sir Walter. *On Novelists and Fiction.* Edited by Ioan Williams. London: Routledge & Kegan Paul, 1968.

Seward, Anna. *The Letters of Anna Seward Written Between the Year 1784 and 1807.* Edited by A. Constable. 6 vols. Edinburgh 1811.

Shenstone, William. *The Letters of William Shenstone.* Edited by Marjorie Williams. Oxford: Basil Blackwell, 1939.

Stewart, Dugald. *Elements of the Philosophy of the Human Mind,* vol 2. *The Collected Works of Dugald Stewart.* Edited by Sir William Hamilton. Edinburgh, 1854.

Trapp, Joseph. *Lectures on Poetry.* London, 1742.

Twining, Thomas. "On Poetry Considered as an Imitative Art." In *Eighteenth-Century Critical Essays.* Edited by Scott Elledge vol. 2. Ithaca, N. Y.: Cornell University Press, 1961.

Warton, Joseph. *An Essay on the Genius and Writings of Pope.* 2 vols 5th ed. London, 1806.

[Whately, Richard.] Review of *Northanger Abbey* and *Persuasion. Quarterly Review* 24(1821):352–76.

Williams, Ioan, ed. *Novel and Romance 1700–1800: A Documentary Record.* London: Routledge & Kegan Paul, 1970.

Wordsworth, William. *Literary Criticism.* Edited by Paul M. Zall Lincoln, Neb.: University of Nebraska Press, 1966.

THEORETICAL AND CRITICAL BACKGROUND:
SECONDARY SOURCES

Abrams, Meyer. *The Mirror and the Lamp: Romantic Theory and the Critical Tradition.* New York: Oxford University Press, 1953.

Alkon, Paul K. *Samuel Johnson and Moral Discipline.* Evanston, Ill.: Northwestern University Press, 1967.

Amarasinghe, Upali. *Dryden and Pope in the Early Nineteenth Century. A Study of Changing Literary Taste, 1800–1830.* Cambridge: University Press, 1962.

Arthos, John. *The Language of Natural Description in Eighteenth-Century Poetry.* University of Michigan Publications, Language and Literature Series, vol. 24. Ann Arbor: University of Michigan Press, 1949.

Booth, Wayne. *The Rhetoric of Fiction.* 4th Impression. Chicago and London: University of Chicago Press, 1963.

Boyce, Benjamin. *The Character-Sketches in Pope's Poems.* Durham, N.C.: Duke University Press, 1962.

Bronson, Bertrand H. "The Pre-Romantic or Post-Augustan Mode." *ELH* 20(1953):15–28.

Butt, John. *The Augustan Age.* London: Hutchinson's University Library, 1950.

Clark, A. F. B. *Boileau and the French Classical Critics in England, 1660–1830.* Bibliothèque de la Revue de Littérature Comparée No. 19. Paris: Champion, 1925.

Cruttwell, Patrick. "On *Caleb Williams.*" *Hudson Review* 11(1958):87–95.

Davie, Donald. *Purity of Diction in English Verse.* London: Chatto & Windus, 1952.

Draper, John W. "The Metrical Tale in XVIII-Century England." *PMLA* 52(1937):390–97.

Dumas, D. Gilbert. "Things as They Were: The Original Ending of *Caleb Williams.*" *Studies in English Literature* 6(1966):575–97.

Eland, Rosamund G. "Problems of the Middle Style: La Fontaine in Eighteenth-Century England." *Modern Language Review* 66(1971):731–37.

Elledge, Scott. "The Background and Development in English Criticism of the Theories of Generality and Particularity." *PMLA* 62(1947):147–82.

Hagstrum, Jean. *Samuel Johnson's Literary Criticism.* Chicago and London: University of Chicago Press, 1967.

———. *The Sister Arts. The Tradition of Literary Pictorialism and English Poetry from Dryden to Gray.* Chicago: University of Chicago Press, 1958.

Jack, Ian. *Augustan Satire. Intention and Idiom in English Poetry, 1660–1750.* Oxford: Clarendon Press, 1952.

Keast, W. R. "The Theoretical Foundations of Johnson's Criticism." *Critics and Criticism Ancient and Modern.* Edited by Ronald S. Crane. Chicago: University of Chicago Press, 1952.

Kroeber, Karl. *Romantic Narrative Art.* Madison: University of Wisconsin Press, 1960.

Kubler, George. *The Shape of Time: Remarks on the History of Things.* New Haven and London: Yale University Press, 1971.

Lawlor, John. "Radical Satire and the Realistic Novel." *Essays and Studies* n.s. 8(1955):58–75.

Leedy, Paul. "Genres Criticism and the Significance of Warton's Essay on Pope." *Journal of English and Germanic Philology* 45(1946):140–46.

McCracken, David. "Godwin's Literary Theory: The Alliance Between Fiction and Political Philosophy." *Philological Quarterly* 49(1970):113–33.

MacKee, William. *Elizabeth Inchbald, Novelist.* . . . Washington, D.C.: Catholic University of America, 1935.

MacLean, Kenneth. *John Locke and English Literature of the Eighteenth Century.* New Haven: Yale University Press, 1936.

Mack, Maynard. "The Muse of Satire." In *Studies in the Literature of the Augustan Age: Essays Collected in Honor of Arthur Ellicott Case.* Edited by Richard C. Boys. Ann Arbor: George Wahr Publishing Co. for the Augustan Reprint Society, 1952.

Miles, Josephine. *Eras and Modes in English Poetry.* Berkeley and Los Angeles: University of California, 1957.

————. "The Romantic Mode in Poetry." *ELH* 20(1953):29–38.

Miner, Earl. "From Narrative to 'Description' and 'Sense' in Eighteenth-Century Poetry." *Studies in English Literature* 9(1969):471–87.

Monk, Samuel H. *The Sublime: A Study of Critical Theories in XVIII-Century England.* New York: Modern Language Association of America, 1935.

Monro, D. H. *Godwin's Moral Philosophy: An Interpretation of William Godwin.* London: Oxford University Press, 1953.

Myers, Mitzi. "Godwin's Changing Conception of *Caleb Williams.*" *Studies in English Literature* 12(1972):591–628.

Paulson, Ronald. *Satire and the Novel in Eighteenth-Century England.* New Haven and London: Yale University Press, 1967.

Randolph, M. C. "The Structural Design of the Formal Verse Satire." *Philological Quarterly* 21(1942):368–84.

Rogerson, Brewster. "The Art of Painting the Passions." *Journal of the History of Ideas* 14(1953):68–94.

Smith, Elton E. *William Godwin.* Twayne's English Authors. New York: Twayne, 1966.

Sutherland, James R. *English Satire.* Cambridge: University Press, 1958.

Sutherland, William O. S., Jr. *The Art of the Satirist: Essays on the Satire of Augustan England.* Austin: University of Texas Press, 1965.

Swedenberg, Hugh T. *The Theory of the Epic in England, 1650–1800.* University of California Publications in English, vol. 15. Berkeley and Los Angeles: University of California Press, 1944.

Tillyard, E. M. W. *The English Epic and its Background.* London: Chatto & Windus, 1954.

Tompkins, J. M. S. *The Popular Novel in England 1770–1800.* Lincoln, Neb.: University of Nebraska Press, 1961.

Trickett, Rachel. *The Honest Muse: A Study in Augustan Verse.* Oxford: Clarendon Press, 1967.

Tuveson, Ernest L. *The Imagination as a Means of Grace: Locke and the Aesthetics of Romanticism.* Berkeley: University of California Press, 1960.

Weinbrot, Howard D. *The Formal Strain: Studies in Augustan Imitation and Satire.* Chicago: University of Chicago Press, 1969.

Wellek, René. *The Later Eighteenth Century.* Vol. 1: *A History of Modern Criticism, 1750–1950.* New Haven: Yale University Press, 1955.

Wilkinson, Andrew M. "The Decline of English Verse Satire in the Middle Years of the Eighteenth Century." *RES* n.s. 3(1952):222–33.

Wimsatt, W. K. "The Augustan Mode in English Poetry." *ELH* 20(1953):1–14.

INDEX